REMINISCENCES

OF THE

EARLY DAYS

OF

FORT WORTH

BY

CAPT. J. C. TERRELL

1906
TEXAS PRTG. CO.
FORT WORTH

Reprinted by TCU Press in cooperation with
Texas Wesleyan University, on the occasion of
Fort Worth's Sesquicentennial Celebration, 1999.

INTRODUCTION.

These reminiscences, rescued from loss by the family scrap-book, are more especially published to please those who knew the people and the incidents of our Fort Worth frontier times.

Should this object be attained the writer will be gratified.

He dedicates this little book to the pioneers of Tarrant County and to their decendants.

J. C. TERRELL.

INDEX.

ILLUSTRATIONS.

CAPT. J. C. TERRELL AND GRANDSON.

Capt. J. C. Terrell landed in Fort Worth in the early 50's, and this is a sketch of his second law office, which he has had removed to his elegant residence on the Southwest Side, as a kind of souvenir of these old days. This building was removed from Birdville, the former County seat. Like Col. Smith, he is still looking backward to the time when Fort Worth was a baby, and he acted as one of the fathers of the foundling. The artist kodaked this as it

CAPT. J. C. TERRELL'S SECOND LAW OFFICE AND CAPT M B LOYD'S
FIRST BANK.

stood to show the *then* with the *now*. Capt. Terrell laid the foundation of successful life in this old building, and we cannot chide him for the remembrance of his old friend. Capt. M. B. Loyd opened his bank in this building March 1, 1873, and he has continued in this business from that day until this, being now president of the First National Bank.

Captain Joseph Christopher Terrell was born in Sumner County, Tenn., October 29, 1831, while his father's family was en route from Virginia to Missouri to seek a new home. His people are Virginians, of Quaker descent. His father, Dr. C. J. Terrell, died the year after settling at Booneville, Cooper County, Mo., and it was there he was reared. He studied law under his eldest brother, Alexander W. Terrell, then at St. Joseph, Mo., but now of Austin, Tex., one of the oldest of the old Texans, and late United States Minister to Turkey under Cleveland's last administration. At the early age of 20, Young Joe joined the Argonauts in quest of golden fleece on the Pacific slope. For five years he floated around in California and Oregon, a child of fortune, without realizing all he expected, for the memory of his dear old mother haunted him, and so he made for the Old Dominion and old associations. This was in 1856. In 1857, he again turned his face towards the Pacific coast, but took in his brother at Austin. After a brief visit there, in February, 1857, he was passing through this, the then hamlet of Fort Worth, on his way back to California, and here met his old school fellow, Dabney C. Dade, now of Springfield, Mo. This settled his destiny. They were not long forming the law partnership of Terrell & Dade, which continued here till the beginning of the Civil War. Dade went back North. Terrell, though voting against secession, did an act which commends his love for his native Southland stronger than in ordinary cases of patriotism— he sided with his people, under the motto, "My country— may she ever be in the right; but, right or wrong, my country." He recruited a company here in this place and marched down Main street—such of it as was in existence then—and joined Waller's battalion as Company F, in Green's cavalry brigade of Confederate troops. He took part in the many battles of his command on this side of the great river, mainly in Louisiana and Texas, and came back here with the remnant of his war-worn veterans, and began life anew at the bottom rung of the ladder. He is an optimist, and ever finds more to laugh at than weep over, well remembering what another has written, "Laugh, and the world laughs with you; but weep, and you weep alone." He is president of the Old Settlers' Association of Tarrant County.

C. C. CUMMINGS.

KILLING HOGS IN FORT WORTH AND THE EARLY DAYS.

"They tell me that I am the oldest real estate owner in the city. The corner of First and Main streets has been mine for forty-eight years. Here, three years before the Civil War, with the aid of a whipsaw, my schoolmate and partner, Dabney C. Dade and myself, built a law office—one-story frame building, with brick chimneys at each end and an open passageway. Here Dade and myself had our bachelor home; slept in one room, law office in the other—hunting and fishing implements mixed with law papers and books scattered around.

"Tarrant County then voted about 700—two terms of District Court a year, limited to one week. My law office was here until 1870. M. T. Johnson, Dade, J. P. Smith and myself voted with Gen. Sam Houston against secession, which only carried in this county by twenty-seven majority. Dade was then District Attorney. He refused to take the oath to the Confederacy, resigned, and went to Springfield, Mo., where he now lives. I accepted from Judge Divine the office of Confederate receiver—after a while resigned and raised a cavalry company—Company F, Waller's Battalion, Green's Brigade—started to the war from this corner and served to the end, then returned and resumed business at the old stand. It was here I had my first home. My oldest child was born here, corner First and Main streets.

"There was no hog law then. I built a smokehouse and killed ten hogs, averaging 225 pounds each, bought a butcher's cleaver and block, smoked and saved the meat and made two barrels of soft soap. No miser ever gloated over hoarded gold as I did over that wealth of meat. I never dreamed of parting with any of it, although there were only three of us in the family. I was 39 years old when I married, and had for several years been fed in boarding houses, and wanted a full meathouse, hence I grieved to sell meat or lard. The pleasures of married life and of peace can only be fully realized by old men and soldiers."

E. M DAGGETT.

LOOKING BACKWARD.

In 1857 I left Austin and came to Fort Worth in company with Col. M. T. Johnson, Dr. (afterward Governor) J. W. Throckmorton, Charley De Morse of the Clarksville Standard, and a young attorney from Virginia named Jordan, who located in Parker County. The Fort then had some 300 inhabitants, nearly all white, and mostly of the border States—that is, from States bordering on Mason and Dixon's line. This county, and a long strip of territory north of Johnson and south of Denton County, constituted "Peter's Colony," an emigration company chartered by the young State of Texas, managed by Hedgecoke, with headquarters in Louisville, Ky. Under the act of the 26th of August, 1857, known as the pre-emption law, this country was open for location, survey and settlement by actual settlers. I came, a young lawyer, to grow up with the country. The nearest railroad was over 200 miles distant. Owing to the liberal homestead provisions in the Constitution of 1845, since made more liberal and definite by the Constitution of 1876, a superior class of early settlers were attracted hither. Business men who had failed in other States came here with the remnants of their fortunes and secured homes and property free from the writ of scire facias. It was not unusual to meet higher culture in a cabin and to see pianos on dirt floors. As a rule, the foreigner settled in the North, then, objecting to our "peculiar instaitution."

As for a law office, none was to be had for love or money. I hired a man named John Branon, and in a few weeks had a two-room office building, with chimneys, on the corner of First and Main streets. The timbers were cut with a whipsaw. Office in one end—sleeping room in the other—and the "hall' was used for saddle, fishing tackle, etc. Hospitality was only 30c per gallon, with corn stoppers. This property I yet own.

Judge Dabney C. Dade, now of Springfield, Mo., and who formerly had been secretary for Gov. Joe Lane, first Governor of Oregon, came also in 1857. He had been my schoolmate, and we became law partners. Both were bachelors; society was decidedly exclusive. The sexes were divided in meeting, sitting on opposite sides of the house, the women with "heads covered," but with no chicken or bird feathers on their bonnets.

Being strangers, we made poor progress in making our way with the girls, and so, tiring of hunting, fishing and of Oldhams & White's digest, and of the long Sundays, and as we both loved Sunday school, I suggested to Dabney that we start one and break the social ice. He boarded with Mrs. W. T. Ferguson; I, with Mrs. Lawrence Steel, where the concrete hotel afterward stood. Dabney was a "disciple of the Christian order," and on occasion could pray and "pitch and carry a tune." It seems to me that the girls were prettier then. Their meek eyes and bright faces haunt me still, and then, their dresses were of reasonable length. Oh! the halcyon days of youth! Melodions, stately organs and pretty soloists appeared afterward to help us worship God. As for myself I was "unattached," but gave valuable service teaching the Bible class; was well up in faiths, baptisms, and was specially versed in Revelations. We bought a desk and books and subscribed for Sunday School Union literature. We had a prosperous and profitable time, broke the ice and got acquainted with the girls, and Sundays became too short then. And thus the establishment of our first Sunday school in Fort Worth.

Of course, when the real "cloth" appeared, Dabney and myself retired from office, but stuck to the Sunday school as the "nursery of the church."

Bill Seburn's Conversion.

Had Clarence S. Darrow witnessed reconstruction in the South, he would more fervently deprecate nearly all penal laws and "Resist Not Evil" would perhaps be a stronger book.

In 1867, when a pocket pistol constituted the most important part of every Southern gentleman's attire, and when excellent Robertson County (Kentucky) goods, supplemented with Tuck Boaz' and Jud Roland's moonshine, sold in our markets overt at a reasonable figure, every man was a law unto himself. While ordinarily human life was held rather cheaply, lynch law, for aggravated offenses for many reasons necessarily and rightfully obtained. Justice did not travel with leaden feet, and taxes were nominal. Two crimes were never condoned—theft of horses and disturbance of religious worship. They were severely punished, without the benefit of clergy.

There then lived on Village Creek, in Tarrant County, one Bill Seburn, a large man with a heart as big as a court house. He had been a good soldier, was freckle-faced, with sorrel, bushy hair. He occasionally indulged. His truth was found at the bottom of a bottle, and when Bill so found it he invariably exploded with voice and pistol, not to injure, but merely to celebrate. He then became unto himself a small Fourth of July.

An old-fashioned Southern Methodist camp meeting, led by Capt. (Rev.) W. G. Veal, afterwards first commander of R. E. Lee Camp, was being held at Henderson Springs, on Village Creek. Early Sunday morning found me there. A large brush arbor and a number of tents and wagons argued a big meeting. From near a grove a man mysteriously beckoned me to approach. I cautiously obeyed, and when he turned I recognized Bill, who appeared with a day-before-yesterday haggard look, and with troubled face and averted eyes, he slowly said: "Cap, yesterday at the Fort, at old Ed. Terrell's, I tanked up on whisky and started home with a full bottle. Passing here I saw two or three men and a lot of women holding a prayer meeting. I rode under the arbor, and just for fun shot into the brush overhead. I don't remember exactly, but my wife told me all. Oh, it is awful! What shall I do?" I told him that from a legal view there was no hope, that no one was ever acquitted in Texas of that crime proven. I asked him what church his wife belonged to. With a deprecatory nod toward the camp he answered: "That shebang over there." Seeing that he was contrite and enhungered, I advised him to about-face on his sins and join that church. Looking quickly up, as with newly inspired hope, he answered, "You reckon ?"

The day meeting was not a success, but at night, after a "powerful sermon" from the text, "The harvest is passed, the summer is ended, and I am not saved," succeeded by a prayer from a gifted woman, in a wierd and shrill voice, uncapping hell and dwarfing Dante's "Inferno" itself, and a call for mourners with the hymn, "Show Pity, O, Lord; O, Lord, Forgive." Imagine my surprise at seeing Bill approach the altar, followed by neighbors and happy brethren. The very biggest brand had been snatched from the burning.

Bill proved true to his vows, is now in the Panhandle of glorious Texas, with cattle on a hundred hills, and is begirt with numerous children.

Justice Grimsley took no cognizance of the offense. The grand jury failed to indict. Hence Poe, mentor of the Cross Timbers, stood mute, and I lost a fee. "So let the Lord be thanked."

Concerning Sam Houston.

In 1857 Gen. Sam Houston, while yet a member of the United States Senate, ran for Governor of Texas against Hardin R. Runnels, the Democratic nominee, whose competitor in convention was M. T. Johnson of Tarrant County. Many of Houston's friends were alienated from him because of his presenting in the Senate the famous preachers' petition, calling them "10,000 vice-regents of heaven," for the abolition of slavery in the District of Columbia and in the forts, arsenals and dock yards of the United States. Runnels was rather an ordinary man, a large slaveholder. He beat Houston 8,924 votes out of a total of 56,190. Two years thereafter Houston beat Runnels for the same office by about 6,000 votes. This was on the eve of secession, and Houston was a pronounced Union man.

In 1860, Houston being Governor, Texas, by about a two-thirds vote, seceded from the Federal Union. The Legislature and the secession convention were in session at Austin at the same time. Gen. Houston and his secretary of state, Mr. Cave, refused to support the new Governor, and were deposed. Houston died in Huntsville in 1863, of a broken heart. During his administration Col. John P. Smith and myself were in Austin on private business. We both voted against secession and were enthusiastic admirers of the Governor. On his invitation, Peter and I spent several days in the executive office in the old Capitol. He saw that we loved him, and even greatness covets admiration. He was a born ruler of men, over six

A. G WALKER

feet two inches tall, straight as an arrow and modeled like a kingly Adonis. He was kind and considerate to all, especially so to young men; dressed plainly, wore a broadbrim wool hat, with a fawnskin waistcoat and walked with cane of his own making. He was an inveterate whittler, and presented W. B. Tucker and myself with souvenirs of his handiwork. He was a great admirer of Gen. Andrew Jackson, his political father, whom I well remember, hav-

ing been presented to him by my grandfather in 1845, the
year he died. My grandfather was a Whig, and an army
contractor in the war of 1812. He would never silently
hear Jackson abused, saying that "patriotism ranks poli-
tics."

Gen. Houston belonged to the Baptist Church, and in looking at this grand, benevolent and godlike man, it was not
hard to realize that he traveled 700 miles from his Indian
home to cane Congressman Stanberry in Washington, who
had slandered him, and this with the consent of a Tennessee
delegation, including James K. Polk, afterward President.

Tarrant County Seat Fight.

These were the halcyon days of young manhood to Peter
Smith and myself, both being of the same age. We were in
Austin when the Fort Worth and Birdville County seat
question, thought to be settled, was again sprung by Col.
A. G. Walker, Senator from this county. Walker was a
client of mine, a native of Virginia, and came to Peter's
Colony from Kentucky. He had been a school teacher and
district surveyor; a good citizen, though pertinacious even
to stubbornness; he never surrendered nor yielded a point.
Dr. J. W. Throckmorton of Collin County, afterward Governor, was Fort Worth's leading friend in the House. This
question had cost the life of more than one good man, and
the State in legislation, $30,000. When the question was
sprung I was booked for a masquerade ball and was to
personify a Franciscan monk. I was adapted for that roll,
having even then a clearing on my head, and my rotund
figure was suggestive of a monastic life. But, hearing
from Peter that the county question was to be heard that
night by the joint committee, the ball as to me was rele-
gated, and Peter and I delved into a cart full of legislative papers from this county and held up the hands of our
noble leader, M. T. Johnson against Walker and Dr. B. F.
Barclay. The committee sat nearly all night and reported
a compromise bill involving another election, which event-
uated in locating the county seat permanently at Fort
Worth. Requiescat in pace!

M. T. Johnson was the father of Tarrant County, as E.
M. Daggett was the father of Fort Worth, his face being on
our city seal. Both were grand men physically, morally
and mentally. The former weighed 225 pounds, the latter
275. Johnson was physically the strongest man I ever
knew. Neither of them was exemplary or saintly, yet both
were to us old settlers veritable heroes. We loved
them for the manifold good they did, and long years ago
have buried their foibles. Both were good Masons.

After all the pains historians take, how imperfect their
labors! Take these two men and Jonas Harrison, for whom
Harrison County was named. Neither is mentioned in the
"Encyclopedia of the New Southwest," nor in "The Indian Wars and Pioneers of Texas." A lesson to us old ones
of today, who should continue to hew to the line, and if
the future names us commendably, well; if not, we are in
good company.

Local Government After War.

Just after the close of our Civil War, far more cruel and
devastating than other wars, we of Tarrant, like all other
counties, were without any local form of government what-
ever. From former decisions and from the very nature of
things, we knew that de facto government existed with us,
but the people at large were unsettled as to our exact legal
status. For instance, marrying people wanted to know
that a license issued by a de facto county clerk was indeed
and in truth valid. A mistake might be horrible, and might
be irremediable. Civil law must obtain. It was a question of bread and meat to us attorneys. By the reconstruction laws of Congress nearly all the intelligence of the
country was barred from office and disfranchised, hence
we were restricted to the aged and carpetbaggers. So, at
the instance of several good people, Edward Hovenkamp of
Birdville, who had been District Attorney in war times, and
I went to Austin, and there we two held an election
and named a full set of county officers. Arriving in Austin,
I saw Provisional Gov. A. J. Hamilton, my brother's old
law partner, who left Texas in 1861, and was made a Briga-

dier General in the Union Army, but never saw active service. In 1859 he was elected to Congress over Gen. Thomas N.
Waul, who organized Waul's Legion. Texas was then en-
titled to but two members of Congress. Both were fine orat-
ors, the former a rough, the latter a finished ashler. Hamilton
was, by a few votes, beaten for Speaker of the House by Gen.
N. P. Banks, who at Mansfield and Brashear City, La., we
called our "Confederate Quartermaster of subsistence."
Gov. Hamilton gave me a pencil note to his provisional Secretary of State, Judge James Bell, whom I well knew. He
was a native Texan and had been on the Supreme Bench.
We handed the note to Judge Bell, he at once asked for a
list of names for appointment. We retired and returned
him a list. The next morning the Judge handed me the
commissions, signed and sealed. Among them were County
Judge Stephen Terry, County Clerk G. Nance, District
Clerk Louis H. Brown, who was an aged man, his wife
being Miss Patterson of Maryland, sister-in-law of Jerome
Bonaparte, brother of the great Napoleon. Mr. Brown was
an elegant, hospitable gentleman of the old school. He
came here in 1858 with an accomplished family and a few
negroes and settled on Marine Creek. His son, Horatio,
was a member of my company.

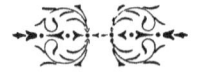

JAMES GRIMSLEY

"THERE WERE GIANTS IN THOSE DAYS"—E. M. DAGGETT AND REV. M. MATTHEWS.

"All nations have a patron saint, and every State its heroes."

The early settlers of Northwest Texas were not without great men. I recall the names of Captain Ephriam M. Daggett and Dr. Mansell Matthews. Both were large men, each weighing about 275 pounds. Both were intellectually great, and were born leaders of men. The face of the former appears upon our city seal, placed there in 1873. Daggett was born in Canada and died here in 1883. He was the leading citizen and one of the founders of Fort Worth. He lived on block B 6, between Main and Houston streets, where he dispensed a feudal hospitality, and where, in 1855, at General Sam Houston's request, he dressed, with his own hands, that old hero's leg that was wounded at the battle of San Jacinto, using the silver basin which Daggett captured from General Santa Anna at the battle of Buena Vista, and which Mrs. Josephine Ryan now owns. He loved our Union, and in 1883 came from near Niagara Falls to the site of Chicago, Illinois, with his mother and his brothers, Henry and Charles, and Mrs. W. M. McKee, all of whom, aged and respected, died in this county. He came to the Republic of Texas in 1840. A Unitarian in belief, he loved the "Mother Church," and gave to the Catholics the land upon which their stone church building stands. He was captain of a company of Texas volunteers in the Mexican war, and served with distinction with Colonel (Captain) Jack Hayes, whom I knew in 1852 in San Francisco. In 1861 he voted for the ordinance of secession, which carried in Tarrant County by a majority of only 27 out of 800 voted polled; D. C. Dade and M. T. Johnson being defeated, and Nathaniel Terry (formerly Lieutenant Governor of Alabama), and Josiah Cook, of Birdville, being elected delegates to the State Convention which deposed Governor Sam Houston and passed the ordinance of secession.

Dr. Mansell Matthews was a highly educated physician, of courtly presence, a Christian preacher without a superior in all our Southland. He had been County Judge of Red River County, and President of the Board of Land Commissioners. He and Daggett belonged to the Masonic chapter here, and were bosom friends. Matthews was a Union man, too outspoken for his personal safety. He was a veritable patriarch of the olden times, and annually traveled with his family, some forty in number, including slaves, camping out, from Red River County to near Austin, some 250 miles. There were no Indians and few fences, to obstruct his march. He would return in the Spring with the rising of grass, with flock and herd. He practiced his profession, but seldom charged for services. His was a nomadic nature, and when on the move his outfit was like a caravan of the great desert. People came from thirty to forty miles to hear him expound the Word and receive his advice. Above all, his genial good nature built up and strengthened the Christian order all along the frontier. He was not a politician; loved the South, but made no secret of his Union sentiments. As sectional hatred intensified, the doctor's real trouble commenced. We then had a civil government in Texas, which existed only in name. The criminal law was as much in the hands of vigilance committees as was that of China in the hands of the Boxers; but I must say it was rarely abused. It would not do for the South to be torn by internal dissentions. She could not afford to guard Valandighams with troops needed at the front. The high vigilance committee court was held in Gainesville, Cook County, and Dr. Matthews was, by its capias, imprisoned there for trial, charged with treason to the Confederate States of America. Constant Dodson presided as judge. The "Overt Act" clause concerning treason, in the State Constitution, had been changed by legislative action, by law of December 14, 1863, making convictions easier by new definitions of the crime. The penalty was death, and few accused escaped. Over a score of his fellow-prisoners, no more guilty than himself, were hung near and in plain view of his prison, on an elm tree. Daggett got word from Matthews, and, obeying his "mark," appeared before the terrible tribunal in his behalf; told them that Matthews had committed no overt act of treason; that his heart was with the South, his mind with the North; that if they hung Matthews they must hang him, too. Matthews was acquitted of the death penalty, but punished by imprisonment for three days, and he was, by way of further punishment, to receive no word of his acquittal during that time. Daggett was allowed to see the prisoner, but only in the presence of the death guard, and was strictly enjoined not to tell the prisoner of the action of the court. Daggett, however, determined that Dr. Matthews should know that his life was saved, and told him so in this way. He talked for over two hours on the subject of death, the immortality of the soul, of repentance, faith, predestination, and especially on the absolute necessity of baptism by immersion as a condition precedent to salvation, etc., etc., etc. This was an unheard of thing for Daggett to do, and his distressed friend wondered what he meant. Of course, Matthews' nerves were strung, and he was intensely on the *qui vive*, knowing that something ulterior was meant by Daggett. Now the guard, from the long, dry talk on the Bible, became listless and inattentive, when Daggett asked Matthews what verse in the Bible afforded him the greatest comfort at this time, and in turn Matthews asked Dagget the same question, to which Dagget replied: "Fret not thy gizzard, and frizzle not thy whirligig, thou, soul, art saved." Matthews asked him to give chapter and verse of the quotation, which, of course, he could not do. After some other conversation the doctor asked him to repeat the verse, the doctor significantly bowing his head, knowing that his life was saved, but that his friend was forbidden to tell him so. He slept soundly that night. Daggett remained in Gainesville three days, and restored Matthews to his family on Deer Creek, in this county. The above incident I had from the lips of both parties."

EDWARD HOVENKAMP.

PRANKS OF LAWYERS—AFTERWARDS JUDGE J. W. FERRIS AND COL. JOHN C. M'COY.

"Should auld acquaintance be forgot,
And never thought upon,
The flames of love extinguish'd
And freely past and gone?"

A copy of Hartley's Digest, a lignumvitae inkstand, pen and handle, a good mustang and lariat—these were necessary implements of trade for an attorney-at-law in Texas in the fifties. The three-ring circus with clown attachment would cease to attract if it had every month in the year. Our great times were few. District Court held only twice a year, and the great time was the annual coming together of attorneys at Austin when the legislature and the Supreme Court were in session at the same time. Then, too, we had business at the general land office, now nearly functus officio. Nearly all traveled by private conveyance, stage-coach conveniences being limited to a few favored localities. The great stage artery of Texas north and south passed through Sherman, McKinney, Dallas, Waxahachie, Waco, Austin and San Antonio.

Colonel John C. McCoy of Dallas in 1857 was District Attorney of the old Sixteenth Judicial District. Mac was a large, jovial man, a good lawyer, and the very prince of good fellows; a practical joker, a firm believer, though unattached. J. W. Ferris of Waxahachie was one of the best attorneys in the state, a man of finished education and address, tall and slender, of Pharaoh's lean kine, and was extremely nervous. He was a man of staid dignity and was a member of the "Church South." He it was who rendered the famous International & Great Northern railroad decision, having been appointed by Governor Coke because of an evenly divided supreme bench.

In the early days the visiting bar arrived on horseback in Weatherford one hot Saturday evening and bathed in the

Clear Fork just north of Carter's mill. Roses and ferns lined the banks and the water was beautifully clear—a dry branch there now.

McCoy and Ferris were warm personal friends, though wholly unlike each other. McCoy that evening was in high glee, and gathering the resisting naked Ferris in his strong arms, proceeded to give an anatomical lecture, using Ferris as a subject, commencing at the frontis and ending at the pedal extremities, Ferris wriggling and exclaiming in vain, "Unhand me, sir! I will hold you personally responsible," etc. Governor Throckmorton, Nat M. Burford, Charley De Morse, M. Hawkins, Amaziah Bradshaw, John C. Easton, John J. Good, Joe Carroll and others enjoyed the fun.

The following winter Colonel McCoy, journeying from Dallas to Austin in a large Concord coach one cold winter night, arrived in Waxahachie. It was pitch dark and the coach was full, but Ferris managed in the dark to crowd into a seat just opposite to McCoy, their knees touching. He did not recognize his tormentor of last spring. Several times when the wheels would run over rocks or ruts McCoy would cry out in pain, violently rubbing his knees. After awhile Ferris being nervous, became uneasy, and exclaimed "Sir, you seem to be quite nervous." Mac answered with an ugly word, "Anyone would be nervous to have two daggers pierce his knees." The Judge indignantly stopped the coach and took a seat on the outside with the driver. At the breakfast-stop he recgnized his tormenter and resumed his seat inside. He forgave, but never forgot.

* * *

The judge often played even with Mac. On one occasion they were leading counsel on opposite sides of an important land case. Mac was for the plaintiff, and gave as his thought the statutory three days' written notice of his intention to read his several muniments of title in evidence. In a list of several conveyances he had omitted one. After consuming several hours in reading his title papers, Mac offered in evidence the omitted deed. Ferris objected

and of course was sustained by the court. Turning, and
politely bowing to Mac, Ferris said: "My jokes, though
practical, are strictly legal and always pay." Of course
the plaintiff broke down, but on payment of costs was granted a new trial.

                "A little nonsense now and then
                 Is relished by the wisest men."

Just after the Civil War, when the country was full of
cattle, then in great demand, the hotel, here in Fort
Worth, was full of cattle buyers from the North, with lots
of money. Strangers to us they were and to each other,
waiting for the grass to rise. They were an uncommuni-
cative set and all dressed with the regulation six-shooter.
There were only three home boarders at the hotel—Ben
Bedford, Walter A. Huffman and myself. Judge Ferris
spent a few days at the hotel preparing his cases for District Court commencing the following Monday. He had
just returned from his first trip North, and day after day
at the dinning table recounted over and over to admiring
listeners his impressions of Niagara Falls and so forth.
One day at dinner with an effort I got the floor first and told
the Judge that I, too, had just returned from a trip from
inside the enemy's lines, that when I got to Galveston I
rode on a great squatty coach that ran on iron rails and
about fifty people were hauled on it by two small mules.
The Judge, talking from his boots, remarked: "Yes, yes—
street car." I answered, "Yes, that is what they called it."
Continuing, I told him that returning home I missed the
connection at Louisville and stopped over at the Gault
House, that they took me into a little room, carpeted, and
with a sofa in it, that a man pulled a rope and, up, up I went
without a jar. The Judge remarked, "An elevator." I
answered "Yes, that is what they called it." Continuing, I
told him that a man lit a match on sand-paper on the wall
in the dark hall and unwound a piece of iron like a coffee-
mill handle, touched the lighted match to it, and behold,
from the very iron sprang a most brilliant light. The Judge
remarked, "That was gas." I remarked, as I rose hastily
from the table, "Yes, Judge, that is exactly what they called

it." As I retreated, those hitherto silent cowmen howled and howled. I got half way across the square before the Judge from the porch called me back. I tried to explain, but it wouldn't wash.

J SAMUEL, J. C. TERRELL AND SAM WOODY.

STORY OF REV. JOHN DENTON AFTER WHOM DENTON COUNTY, TEXAS WAS NAMED.

Dr. Ash N. Denton died at his residence in Austin on the 6th instant.

This announcement awakened memories long dormant. In 1858, while an orphan boy, Denton lived in Weatherford. A saloonkeeper there, named Big Jim Curtis, abused him, a fight with revolvers ensued, resulting in Curtis' death. Denton obtained a change of venue and was tried and acquitted in Buchanan, then the county seat of Johnson County. Denton came to Fort Worth, where he was elected Justice of the Peace; commenced reading law with A. Y. Fowler, but afterwards studied medicine with Dr. Calvin M. Peak, the son of Captain Peak, the Mexican war veteran of Dallas County, and graduated in Galveston medical school in 1861. He was married here to a most beautiful and accomplished lady, Miss Maggie Murchison, who survives him. He located at or near San Marcos; from there he moved to Austin and took charge of the insane asylum as superintendent during Governor Ireland's two administrations. In 1898, I with my two brothers, called on ex-Governor F. M. Lubbock, who was sick. Doctor Denton was his physician, and I saw him there for the last time.

The following I state from memory, told me by John C. McCoy, deceased, of Dallas. McCoy was surveyor of the Peters Colony company in the days of the Republic of Texas and was afterward District Attorney of the Sixteenth Judicial District.

Denton County was named in honor of Captain John R. Denton, the father of Dr. Ash Denton. He was a most remarkable man, an attorney, a Methodist preacher and a distinguished Indian fighter; was killed by the Comanche Indians on Rush Creek, this county, near where the Texas and Pacific Railroad crosses that stream. McCoy said that he never heard his equal as an orator. For a frivolous cause he separated from his wife in Arkansas. She went to Fayetteville and there established a little millinery store. One night a merchant, a man of wealth and local influence, on attempting to enter her room, was shot and killed by Mrs. Denton. She was indicted for murder and imprisoned. It was generally thought that on account of the influence of the prosecution and of the desperado friends of the deceased Mrs. Denton would be convicted. On the day of the trial the court room was densely crowded with spectators. The presiding judge asked the defendant if she had an attorney to defend her. She answered: "No; I have no attorney and no friends." A stranger to all, sitting inside the bar arose, gazing intently into her face, said: "No, not without friends. If it please your honor, I will appear for the defendant, if acceptable to her and to the court."

She recognized her husband in the stranger, who, being unknown, exhibited his license to the court, and the trial proceeded. The facts were plain. Her counsel seemed abstracted and asked the prosecuting witnesses but few pertinent questions. The State's attorney, an able advocate, made a strong effort, and many trembled for the fate of the beautiful defendant. When he had finished his opening address Denton arose to reply. He discussed the law of murder in its various degrees, and the law of self-defense as applicable to the evidence in the case. In manner he was as calm, cool and emotionless as if he were an animated marble statue. But every point he made was as clear as the noonday sun, and he spoke as he shot—to the center every time. And his very impassiveness seemed to carry conviction. The first emotion he displayed was in his peroration, when, resting his eyes upon the defendant, he said in part: "Gentlemen of the Jury, look upon the defendant. Scan that pure face and behold something dearer to me than life, and more precious to me than all things else under the blue canopy of heaven. Need I tell you that she is my wife. I could as easily believe an angel guilty of crime as my wife. She never had an impure thought in her life. It is true that whilst no woman was ever gentler or more kind-hearted or more faithful and affectionate wife, she, with a courage born of virtue and innocence, slew the ruffian who would have desecrated my fireside. And for this worthy deed of a noble woman I honor and love her more than ever. Thank God for having blessed me with such a wife."

Concluding, he advanced toward the defendant, and, exclaimed: "No, not without a friend, little woman," and, extending his arms, "behold in me you have more than a friend—a husband!"

She sprang to his breast amid the tears and acclaims of the people and the cries of the sheriff for "order in the cuort!" The jury, looking to the right and left and talking to each other, without leaving their box, returned instanter a verdict of "Not guilty." The friends of the prosecution were immediately conspicuous by their absence.

Captain Denton and wife then moved to Clarksville, Texas. A full account of this trial was published over forty years ago by Charley De Morse in his Clarksville Standard.

GIDEON NANCE.
Sixteen Years County Clerk.

WEATHERFORD, TEXAS IN THE RECONSTRUC-
TION DAYS.

"Lull'd in the countless chambers of the brain,
Our thoughts are linked by many a hidden chain;
Awake but one, and lo, what myriads rise!
Each stamps its image as the other flies."

A few days ago, accompanied by two dark horses and
a number of friends interested in the Congressional convention I found myself in the court house at Weatherford,
Texas, more liberal to Parker than to her other counties,
gave her, at her organization in '56-7, a tract of land on
which Weatherford is built, and with the proceeds of the
sale of lots the county erected quite a handsome brick court
house in the center of the public square, where the present
more pretentious building stands. Our delegation sat in
the center of the court room, and thus was brought "the
light of other days around me."

In the fall of 1859, within a few feet of this spot, there
were suspended from the ceiling several rows of Indian
scalps, with bows, shields, spears, etc., while under and
around, to the time of sweet music, we traced the light
fantastic in many mazy sets. John R. Baylor and his
brother, George, with others, had whipped the Indians;
these scalps, etc., were the proof, and cause of rejoicing,
for Parker County was then often raided by Comanches.
The Civil War ensued, when the frontier was never so
well guarded. It was the least dangerous and most popular service in the Confederacy. Provisional Governor A.
J. Hamilton appointed R. W. Scott, of Johnson County, District Judge. He held the first term of the District Court
for Parker County after the close of the war, in the spring
of 1866. H. H. Sneed was District Attorney, and David
Yeary, foreman of the grand jury. The county officers
were: W. Frank Carter, County Judge; R. W. Duke, County Clerk; Joseph W. Anderson, District Clerk; D. B. Luckey,
Sheriff, and Dr. E. Milliken, Treasurer. The local attor-

neys were: A. J. Hood, Daniel O. Norton, H. S. Coleman,
Simon Sugg, H. H. McLean, C. L. Jordan, A. J. Ball and R.
J. McKenzie. The visiting attorneys were Joe Carroll, J. C.
Easton, Joe Rushing, John J. Goode, Joe Bledsoe, H. G.
Hendricks, Ed. Hovenkamp, J. C. Terrell and M. Hawkins.

Under the advice of that great and good man, General
Sam Houston, peace and plenty reigned in Texas during
the war. Not so in the divided border States. During the
whole struggle criminal laws were uninterruptedly admin-
istered; the laws of limitation were by legislative enactment suspended between the 28th day of January, 1861,
and the 13th day of March, 1870. True, in some sections
vigilance committees, composed, as a rule, of the very best
elderly men, existed. Having neither money, credit nor
manufactories, the people were in a primitive condition.
Health, courage and hope were left. Horses and cattle
upon a thousand hills she had. These could walk to market.
Then, too, she had free grass and no taxation. Soon better
times dawned. The dream which said, "Arise, Peter, slay
and eat," to him a convenient dream, was to our people
a glorious reality. Thousands of unbranded and unclaimed
cattle abounded. Even boys ran branding irons with mar-
velous success.

Soon there was a general desire to resume the reign of
law and order. Norton was appointed Judge of the Sixteenth Judicial District, which embraced Parker County.
He was an old editor, an intelligent, good man, but an indiff-
erent lawyer. He swore in 1844 that he would not shave
his face until Henry Clay was elected president, and kept
his oath. He loved Texas, and was good to Confederate
prisoners in Ohio, and this atoned for many sins. He made
a good officer for the times, which were queer, peculiar
and without precedent. At Norton's first term in Weatherford a Federal lieutenant and a squad of men camped on the
hill west of Carson & Lewis' hotel. The Indians gave some
trouble then, and killed a man on the Clear Fork, between
Weatherford and Fort Worth; hence the attorneys went
from Fort Worth in a body. I remember the following:
M. Hawkins, Henry Sneed, J. C. Easton, E. Hendricks, G.

A. Everetts and Ed. Hovenkamp. The officers then in Parker were Sam Milliken, who was both District and County Clerk; Wes Hendricks, Sheriff; Joe Wilbarger, County Judge, and H. H. Sneed, District Attorney. The local attorneys were Charley Jordan, of Lynchburg, Va.; A. J. Ball, of Kentucky; A. J. Hood, E. W. Hughes, Joe Wolfolk and S. W. T. Lanham. I remember being one of a committee of attorneys who examined Lanham in open court on his application for license, and then predicted that he would some day be Governor of Texas. His moral character was so good, his manners so genial, and his answers to questions so prompt and clear, caused us all to love him, who was then the "kid of the bar."

Uncle Jimmy Jones, God bless him, was presiding elder of the Methodist Episcopal Church, South, and on the Sunday preceding court held forth in Ike McConnell's long, dirt-floor school house, located north of the square. Lanham, a devout member of Uncle Jimmy's church, caused the visiting bar to attend the meeting. We sat together. Uncle Jimmy took for his text, "Woe unto you, lawyers, hypocrites;" and instead of applying the text to the house of Levi—his own cloth—he applied it to us attorneys, himself having had a good time "enduring the war." He wanted no courts, and was in favor of the status quo. Note the effect of that sermon! The next day a number of young men, ex-Confederate soldiers, assembled with Enfield rifles on the hill north of town and bombarded the court house square, causing many to hug the south side of the court house. Fortunately no one was hurt.

There was little or no money in the country. I remember collecting a good fee in peltry, buffalo and other hides, which our merchants had no trouble in exchanging for money.

Weatherford has good water, from the same sandstone formation that furnishes our supply, but needs water works sadly. Abounding in good church buildings, schools and residences, with enterprise her future is assured. She has given to Texas our Sam Lanham, and George Clark, now of Waco. May her new generation do as well!

THE ONLY TWENTY DOLLAR FELONY BOND.

No one served the people of Texas with greater honor to the State and himself, as Supreme Judge and Governor, than did the old Alcalde, O. M. Roberts. To some extent he possessed the genius of the great Napoleon in selecting his lieutenants. Among them was John D. Templeton, his Attorney General, a young man of unusual dignity, with a fine legal mind.

It was my good fortune, in 1869, to meet young Templeton in his first case. It was in an examining court in Tarrant County, Texas, James Grimley, Justice. The old practice of "taking" cattle was fast playing out. Defendant owned no cattle but had collected and sold several small herds; was arrested in possession of some forty head, to which he could show no bill of sale. It was a hot spring day. The examination was held in a grove, was largely attended, and nearly every man had his shotgun. It looked squally for the defendant, who paid me all his money, except a twenty dollar gold piece, and gave me a written promise for a set of house logs.

The state proved adverse ownership as to only one animal, a crumpled horn work steer, worth ten dollars, and the defendant was held to answer for the theft of that animal—a felony charge. The question was as to the amount of bail. I contended with simulated gravity that the court should fix the bond at double the amount of the value of that steer; read from the Federal and State Constitutions as to "excessive bail," and from the Statute laws on amounts of bonds in attachment and sequestration cases—double the value in litigation. Uncle Jimmy declared that he once had an attachment case before him and that he would hear evidence as to the value of the steer. All hands adjourned to the yard, where "Aunt Jane" had prepared a good dinner of jerked beef, bread and buttermilk. Court resumed business and fixed the amount of the bond at twenty dollars. The house logs were delivered, and made me a smokehouse. The defendant was finally acquitted.

SAM WOODY   E. S. TERRELL   RICHARD KING
HOWARD PEAK   J. C. TERRELL   DAN PARKER

WHY SAM WOODY LOCKED HIS WAGON WHEELS EVERY NIGHT.

During the period of reconstruction in Texas, returning to Fort Worth from, I think, the last term of the District Court of Johnson County that was held at Buchanan, and arriving at Nolan River, I saw, newly camped there, Sam Woody, of Deep Creek, Wise County. He had about ten yokes of oxen, two or three horses, and two large wagons, which were loaded with goods en route to Fort Worth from Calvert, 200 miles distant, but then our nearest railroad depot.

The weather was warm and the moon being full, I preferred traveling at night, but accepting Sam's pressing invitation, spent the night with him; so, stripped my horse and picketed him with the others.

There was not on all the frontier, a bigger soul or a more companionable man than Sam Woody. One of the first settlers of Wise County, he was raised in the mountains of Tennessee, a neighbor of Governor Bob Taylor. He was fond of the good things of this life, and at home, as in camp, lived like a prince; a man of great piety, his word was his bond. Fond of joking, he never descended to the vulgar, and never exaggerated. Nearly everybody knew him and he was universally beloved.

I noticed that the wheels of his wagons were locked, and asked his negro man the reason. He said he didn't know; that Mass' Sam made him lock the wheels every night, but 'twas mighty strange. Just before passing off to sleep my eyes again caught sight of the locked wheels and of an old horseshoe nailed to the wagon box. This suggested superstition in the owner, that some mysterious connection existed between the horseshoe and the locked wheel. What was it? All men are more or less superstitious, but mountaineers, sailors and frontiersmen are especially so. Without doubt it is caused by solitude, and for the same cause, I take it, such men as Napoleon and Cromwell, compelled to mental isolation, became superstitious. Reflecting thus, while listening to the heavy breathing of the oxen, the crowing of plover and the barking of coyotes, Sam leisurely arose, stretched himself and refilled his pipe. At risk of giving offense I asked why he locked his wheels. Edgar Poe asked questions of the raven and answered them himself. Perhaps I would have to do the same thing. But I was consumed with curiosity. With rather an embarrassed look, after an uproarious laugh, he said in substance:

"Cap, just before the war I went down to Fort Worth with a load of wheat for Field & Man's gristmill, above the blue hole on Clear Fork, and loaded back with domestic, sugar, coffee and one thing and another. A hired man—a tenderfoot—was with me. Seeing that he was getting too full I told him to go to camp across the river, above the junction, and to yoke the oxen to the wagon, and that I would be along directly. He wanted to take the jug, but I retained that in my hand. In an hour or so I went over to the camp. Well, sir, that fellow had hitched up the team, loaded the mess tricks, got up in the wagon, went to sleep, and away the whole chebang marched for Deep Creek. Left with that jug of whisky I was in a fix. It was a full moon, like this. I walked over ten miles before I stopped them, and every mile I swore in good earnest, always hereafter to lock my wheels. When that fellow woke up he said, 'Well, you've come at last?'

"You see, Cap, not being a Catholic, there is no way for me to be absolved from them oaths." I told him that I thought he was wrong. He replied that Bro. W. G. Veal also told him so, but that the Bible says, "Thou shalt make thy prayer unto him, and thou shalt pay thy vows."

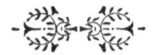

THE FORT WORTH UNIVERSITY.

I was on my way to Virginia, when I met Rev. A. A. Johnson, at that time preaching the gospel and the tenets of John Wesley Methodism in Texas. He said that he had been preaching for two years without a convert, yet he desired to do something for the church by which he could pay back to it the debt he owed for his education as a minister of the gospel. The Methodist Episcopal church had just determined to establish the third of its trinity of educational institutions in the South, the other two having been planted at Chattanooga and Little Rock. He was earnest in the belief that Fort Worth could secure the prize. Why don't you incorporate, I asked him, and not long afterward he came to my office and I drew up the charter.

A few days later I met William H. Cannon, a traveling salesman, and a devout member of the Methodist church, and explained the plan to him, telling him of a piece of land forty acres in extent, in front of my home property that could be bought. Captain John Hanna was the agent for the land, and I advised Johnson to buy it.

The deal was made, and Johnson and Cannon sold enough lots off that forty acres to clear up about $4,000 apiece. They reserved the balance for the campus, gave it to the University and on it the buildings of the institution have been erected. The property thus donated is worth now in the neighborhood of $150,000.

Following the incorporation of the company to build the University, the people here raised $10,000 to help the project along. Captain Lloyd gave $700, Joe Brown $500, W. J. Boaz $500, Peter Smith $500 and others equal amounts. The church put in $10,000 and when the building was completed a debt of $3,000 had been incurred. This the educational association of the general church paid off, and since that time the University has not been encumbered. I have educated five children at the institution. The pictures of Johnson and Cannon hang on the walls of the chapel in grateful remembrance of the services they performed for the University.

NATHANIEL TERRY.

He came to Tarrant County in 1854. He had been the Democratic nominee for Governor in Alabama, defeated by Governor Jones, his brother-in-law, in a three-cornered race. At that time Lieutenant Governors in Alabama were elected by the State Senate. He was twice elected Lieutenant Governor. His defeat for Governor, by an independent candidate, probably made him the strict partisan that he was. His wife, nee Jones, was a refined, educated and lovely woman. Two daughters and two sons, with some thirty-six negroes, constituted the family. These slaves were given to Mrs. Terry by her brother, for the Colonel had failed in business, and eighty of his slaves were sold by the Sheriff under execution. The Colonel had been one of the highest flyers in the Union. Among his assets was Uncle Daniel, his body servant, keeper and rider of Ringgold, a famous horse costing him $3,000. Daniel, with Ringgold, won a great race at Saratoga, when it was safe for a Southern man to travel with his slaves through the North without John Brown's interference. This horse was named after Ringgold, commander of the famous battery which did famous service in Mexico. The horse was a deep sorrel, with heavy mane and tail, and in motion he was a poem. Even at this day I occasionally see the favor of the descendants of this grand horse in this country.

Colonel Terry settled the H. C. Holloway place northeast of this city in 1854. He bought this land from M. T. Johnson. He was a pronounced secessionist, and in 1862 sold his farm to David Snow, an anti-secessionist, for $10,-000,which he took in Confederate money in preference to gold coin offered him. In 1863 the Confederate Congress compelled the funding of this money into bonds, and I fell heir to the same in an iron safe which I bought from Captain M. B. Loyd—the bonds worthless, of course. David Snow, under a dirt floor in the rear of No. 109 Weatherford street in this city, buried $10,000 in gold coin, which he resurrected in 1866. He married a Miss Bradley, daughter of the founder of Camden, Ark., and died there. He was a shoemaker by trade, and made his money by merchandising.

The Colonel's house consisted of a row of several rooms snow white and well furnished, facing the south, fronted with a porch with floors of stone. There were separate apartments for the aged couple. He kept the most hospitable home I ever knew. When Governor Houston, Jack Hamilton, M. P. Wall, A. W. Terrell and other noted men visited the village no one dreamed that they would go to the hotel. Colonel Terry entertained them, as of course, and their friends also.

Utterly ruined by the result of the war, this aged couple died here about the same time. Like Cicero, the Colonel loved and served his country, and lost all by espousing a lost cause.

OLD PAUL TYLER AND HIS DOG "SOUNDER."

The early settlers of Tarrant County were native Americans, almost without exception. As a rule they were pious people, for I cannot recall an irreligious family. The few merchants carried heavy stocks; credit extended for a year, was almost universal, and was rarely abused. A whole chapter by contrast, is contained in this declaration.

The good effects of the Act of August 26, 1856, opening Peters' Colony to pre-emption and settlement, were immediately felt. The Neighborhood of Clarksville, Tennessee, furnished many emigrants, among others, A. D. Johnson, Paul Isbell, James K. Allen, Stephen Terry, James Grant, Jack Collier, the Hagoods, R. H. and William King, the Pettyes, John Weims, John Ingraham, C. G. Payne and Paul H. Tyler, with their servants and household goods, settled in and near Fort Worth.

Paul Tyler was of Falstaffian proportions; weighed 225 pounds, a genial bachelor, over 60 years old. He had been the stay and support of his mother and sisters in Tennessee. Surviving them, he followed his friends and neighbors to Texas. His was a blighted existence. He worshipped Nature and loved the primeval forest, and usually hunted alone. With his gun and rod he was a welcomed inmate of every family. His appearance was ever welcomed, especially by children, whom he dearly loved. His departure caused protest and insistence of early return. But after all, Paul's best friend was his faithful dog, old Sounder, an immensely large Virginia dearhound, a regular blackand tan, large muzzle, a little pepper and salt color on the breast and tip of his tail. He had a deep trailing voice, like the music of distant thunder, oft-repeated. Few realize the importance of a good dog in a new country. Suppose for a moment that the species had not existed; how could man, without the assistance of the dog, have been able to conquer, tame and reduce to servitude every other animal. How could he discover, chase and destroy those that were noxious to him. In order for him to become master, it was necessary for him to begin by making friends of a part of them, to attach such of them to himself by kindness as seemed fittest for obedience and pursuit. Thus the first art employed by man was in conciliating the favor of the dog, and the fruits of this art were the conquest and peaceful possession of the earth. The ancients deified the dog. God created Sounder a deerhound of the purest breed. Paul traced his pedigree through Cumberland Gap to James Kennerly's kennel, in Patrick County, Virginia, near Mayoforge.

In 1859, when Lawrence Steel moved to the White Settlement, Paul and faithful Sounder went, too. More than human love existed between them. Let one of us go to the door, or on the porch, and no Sounder; but let Paul go, and lo, Sounder was there. He fed him on cold, unsalted cornbread, a little peppered. Paul never ate without remembering Sounder. The understanding between them was wonderful. Was a hog to be caught Sounder stood mute and inattentive until Paul spoke, and then success immediately followed obedience. Damon and Pythias could have loved no more. Old Paul's human loves were dead. God gave the old man Sounder to compensate.

One day Sounder was missed. They heard him trailing on the Toombs and Catlett land. The next day Sounder was heard on the trail, and woodmen reported him an hour behind a big buck. That night he came home apparently fagged out, but by sunup of the third day he was on the trail and the woodcutters reported Sounder in sight. By 3 o'clock he bayed the buck in water at the mouth of Silver Creek, where Paul killed it. Mr. Steel again moved; this time to Parker County. Paul and Sounder went, too, and died there near Veals Station. Scientists cannot tell us the line between instinct and intelligence. Certainly Sounder had a spark of intelligence which is immortal.

I believe that Paul and Sounder are reunited in the hunter's Elysium, where Sounder leads the pack, and has dog days to spare. This twain, like Abelard and Heloise, deserve a monument.

C. B. DAGGETT
Owned the First Store in Tarrant County.

MY FIRST HUNT IN TARRANT COUNTY.

When a younger man I loved to hunt and fish. Diana and Izaak Walton were my patron saints. The fact is, my love for these sports had much to do with my locating in Fort Worth. The neighborhood of the Queen City of the Prairies was then the hunter's paradise.

It was in February, 1857. The day was clear, cold and crisp. An ideal Texas midwinter day. Our hunting ground for the day lay in the woods between the "Fort" and Birdville. Deer were numerous; wild turkeys abounded in the bottom; some herds of antelope yet survived on the prairies. The West Fork was over half-bank full, with some drift wood running; no bridge or ferry. So R. H. King and myself went in a skiff down the river from near the site of the long bridge to the brickyard crossing east of town, so as to ferry over the hunters and recross from camp with game on home-coming.

R. H. and William King, C. G. Payne, Paul Tyler and K. Coleman were of the party. R. H. King, now of this city, and then Master of our Masonic lodge, and myself, alone survive.

I had a large shotgun, which chambered four "blue whistlers." When a few hundred yards below the town I stood up in the stern of the boat to better aim at some game, and "all accoutered as I was," fell overboard, holding on to my gun, turned a summersault in the bosom of the deep, saved the gun, and wrung out my clothes just above the Cold Spring; crossed the boys over and separated for the hunt. King and myself killed a fine buck and wounded another, near the Cross Spring, where Uncle Alsie Johnson planted the mint for juleps. Following the hounds, we found the wounded deer in the water at the foot of a steep bank, on the south side of the river, his nose and antlers only showing above the water. William King and myself swam across the river to the buck, King with knife in his mouth. Together we held the deer while King dispatched it. It was a large buck, and we swam across the river with him between us, each holding a prong of his horns. I never had so cold a bath.

In those days whisky was a necessary part of a camp out-fit. We had a good article of Robinson County "goods." The boys drenched us with a double "Timothy," and I felt none the worse for my double bath. No one doubted that Robinson County whisky was nectar for the gods. It is said the Primitive Baptists used it for sacramental purposes. It was delightfully, deliciously enjoyable and "like the dew of Hermon that ran down on Aaron's beard, even to the hem of his garments," it went down smoothly, spontaneously and without combustion, and was immediately felt to the end of the toes, permeating the whole human frame divine with a genial glow which must pe felt to be even remotely understood. They can make no more like that. And think of it! Only thirty cents a gallon, with a red corncob attach-ment.

So long as the firm of "Coleman & Payne's" stock lasted, camp hunts were frequent if not profitable. The product was untaxed in those days of true Democracy.

The decrees of the gods are inscrutable. The past is im-mutable! Who can tell! Some of us believe that if the State administration had used Robinson County whisky alone, the convicted Waters-Pierce Oil Company monopoly would not be doing business in Texas.

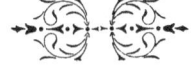

A MOTHER'S LOVE—SWAPPING BABIES.

Standing on the corner of First and Main streets, where Capt. J. C. Terrell, with the aid of a whipsaw, built his law office, 45 years ago, he remarked: "It was just 35 years ago that my oldest child, a girl, was born here. I was glad, but would have been gladder had it been a boy.

"A few months later I was traveling with the young child and its mother, and spent a night at a small clearing in Hill County, where there was a young mother with a beautiful boy baby the age of my girl. The mother was washing under a willow tree, near a spring. Her Cupid crowing on a Mexican blanket spread on the grass.

"I remarked to my wife in a stage whisper, "You know I wanted a boy; let us swap children with this good woman. I will pay its mother, and the children will never know the difference. Wife agreed, and went off with our baby to the house.

"Then I turned to the woman, exposing a handful of gold, and made the proposition to swap, offering more money on my return to Fort Worth. She turned leisurely around, deposited the garment on the wash tub, removed the snuff stick from her mouth, stood at attention, with flushed cheeks, gazing intently into my eyes, remarked slowly, but with dignified emphasis: "Stranger, I would see you in hell first."

Negotiations were indefinitely suspended.

ROBT. TANAHILL,
County Judge

A SHORT SKETCH OF THOS. P. OCHILTREE.

The gallant Major Thomas P. Ochiltree, who recently died in Virginia, was a son of William B. Ochiltree, a distinguished jurist and one of the founders of the Republic of Texas, whither Tom came from Alabama, an infant. When quite a lad he was thrown from a horse, striking his head against a tree, and all of the past became to him a blank. He even had to relearn his A, B, C's. He had good tutors and favorable surroundings and progressing rapidly, became at an early age a good Latin, Spanish and French scholar. It is believed that save the fathers of the Republic, no Texan was more widely known than Tom Ochiltree. He was truly *sui generis,* his life a romance. Comparing Tom with historic characters, whom he somewhat resembled, the name of "Beau" Hickman, who flourished in Washington City about the time of the Mexican War, and of "Beau" Brummell, of George IV time naturally recur; but he was a superior man to either of them, living in a more enlightened age, of gentle lineage, without the advantages possessed by them, a poor man, product of the Texas frontier, he consorted, in peace and in war, with the highest, as a social and intellectual equal, at home alike in palace and in cottage.

I first met him in Austin, Texas, in the winter of '56-7, when he was sergeant-at-arms to the House of Representatives, and often reading clerk. He often called the roll from memory. He was an original secessionist and a member of the Charleston Convention that spoke the Civil War, himself, for one so young a leading actor. His disabilities of minority were removed by special act of the legislature of '57-8, so as to enable him to practice law. His father was his partner; an elderly man, who declined a place in President Davis' cabinet, thus making a way for Judge John H. Reagan. Tom served as a private soldier in Virginia, New Mexico and Louisiana and was for a long time on General Dick Taylor's staff with the rank of major. He was a good Confederate soldier; served as a mere boy in the Texas army against the Indians.

Immediately after the surrender he was imprisoned on Johnson's Island, Lake Erie. Released, he went to Europe; returning, became junior editor of the Houston Telegraph. In '66-7 I saw him in Austin. He asked me what I intended to do. I told him I would practice law. He answered, "There is no law practice. I am going North, where there is some life and lots of money."

He aspired to be special correspondent of the New York Tribune and was strapped, as usual, but managed to get to New Orleans, where he stopped at the St. Charles, of course. There lived then in New Orleans a man named Moody, whose advertisements were as noted in Louisiana, Arkansas and Texas as the Famous Douglass shoe man is today. On every conspicuous place there appeared his sign, "Get your shirts at Moody's," "No. —— Canal street, New Orleans." And so, paying his last dollar for a cab, Tom went to Moody's. Remaining in the cab he sent for Mr. Moody, exhibited his commission as major on General Taylor's staff, introduced himself and went with Mr. Mody to his private office and there demanded his shirts. Mr. Moody sent for the head clerk, who informed him that the major had no shirts there; whereupon Tom said: "Mr. Moody, read that. I wrote it at my rooms at the St. Charles last night. You will observe, sir, that I get from you two trunks, loaded with everything pertaining to a gentleman's wardrobe, from a collar button to a cloak, and $50 in cash to pay my way to New York, and this is your advertisement, worth thousands of dollars."

Mr. Moody carefully read, and after pondering profoundly, replied: "Major, you are right. Select your trunks and clothing, and here is a fifty-dollar check." Now we find Tom in New York at the desk of Horace Greeley. He showed him his commission as major, told him his boy record as editor, and pledged his ability to forward the interests of the Tribune at the World's Fair in Paris, and thanked him for his efforts in President Davis' behalf, the brother-in-law of his late chief. He further said that if his articles

were not received, to cast them into the waste basket and
no charge would be made. Mr. Greeley wrote out and delivered to him the coveted appointment, with which he hied
him to the White House at Washington City and obtained
from General Grant the classmate of General Taylor, a
special pardon—one of the few granted by him, and which
was afterwards questioned by President Johnson. General
Grant also gave him a note to the Secretary of State to com-
mend Major Ochiltree to our ministers in Europe as a
worthy, gallant and meritorious citizen of the United States
of America. Thus armed, he went to Mr. Greeley's banker
in New York, where, on his own note, he borrowed $500.
With all these documents he went to the passenger shipping
offices and found no difficulty in getting free passage to
Paris. Some questions arose as to incidental expenses in-
curred during the passage over, which we will not notice.
He was a man of the world. His brains and knowledge
of men his only capital invested. In Paris he engaged rooms
near the American legation and advertised by a large gold
sign reading thus: "Major Thomas P. Ochiltree, Special
Correspondent of the New York Tribune." Then he is said
to have made and spent many thousands. It is safe to say
that there existed no better judge of horses and dogs than
Tom Ochiltree.

At that time, here in Fort Worth, we had a mail only once
a week. I took the Tribune and eagerly read Tom's contri-
butions, which ever sounded sporty and were easily recognized as genuine. He was an American brick. After the
conclusion of the Paris fair he crossed the channel and was
by our minister at St. James presented to Prince Albert,
now King Edward. It seems that this Prince and Tom saw
horses and dogs alike and there is no doubt they became
chums, and often sailed together on the Prince's private
yacht, and certainly made one voyage around the Isle of
Man. There was some trouble about the Prince's bets
at the derby races, which is said to have led to an estrange-
ment between them.

Returning to Texas, in 1882, was elected to Congress from
the Galveston District and made himself notorious by in-

troducing a resolution commending in strong terms Herr Lasker, a Socialist, who died in Galveston and who had been expelled from Prussia. The resolution, undebated, passed, of course, and gave the world a sensation.

Tom died a bachelor, a Confederate, and a Union patriot. He was true to the Confederacy while it lasted. In the new political shuffle and deal he took a hand with Generals Mahone, Longstreet and others, differing from the mass of his friends. For that matter, so did St. Paul—a personal matter, and we should criticise neither without charity. Tom and St. Paul might both be right.

About the time Tom was in England the boys told some queer tales, showing his standing at court. To illustrate: Once on a grand occasion at Windsor Palace, the Queen, gorgeously attired, was ascending the grand stair, when Tom rather roughly slapped her majesty on the shoulder. Turning with royal indignation and observing Tom, her countenance relaxed into a pleasant smile and she remarked, "O, it is you, Tom."

"The evil that men do lives after them; the good is oft interred with their bones. So let it be with Caesar."

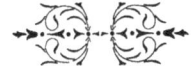

QUININE IN THE SIXTIES.

It has often been said that no generation writes its own history. Dr. Palmer of New Orleans in his great oration at the late Confederate reunion at Louisville repeats this, and in confirmation cites the fact that no full or satisfactory history of the long war between Spain and The Netherlands in the reign of Charles V, was written until after a lapse of three hundred years and that history was penned by a native of another hemisphere.

Some day a Victor Hugo, who wrote the "History of a Crime," or another Motley, in writing dispassionately and from the records concerning our reconstruction period, will tell of the facts of Congress of 1862, 1863, 1864 and 1865, placing a tariff of 45 cents on quinine, raising the tariff from 15 cents under the law of 1857 to 45 cents, and raising the tariff on Peruvian bark from 15 cents in 1846 to 20 cents in 1862 and 1866. Quinine was a medicine of prime necessity in the South, which used twenty times more than the North; and because of this tax and the consequent monopoly of quinine, it retailed in the drug stores in the South at $16 an ounce—its weight in gold. The law prevented importation from Europe and enabled the only manufacturers of the drug in the United States to enjoy a monopoly. The Confederate States being blockaded on the South and invested on the North could only look for an uncertain supply dependent upon blockade runners. This law was repealed in 1868, but the high price obtained practically during the reconstruction, for it was only placed upon the free list in 1868, when its price fell to $1.35 an ounce. This period from 1866 to 1868 marked a time of great poverty and suffering in the South. Negroes, as a class, and poor white people generally, could not buy this drug and resorted to the use of corn shucks, dogwood and willow bark. Hence many thousands died because of the effects of this tax. The South was then unrepresented in Congress, which, had it been advised as to the far-reaching and cruel effects of the law, would doubtless have repealed at the close of the war. John Conness of California (an alien), Thaddeus Stephens and other malignant enemies of the South had it all their own way in Congress. For cold, cruel, hatred and revenge it far exceeded any law enacted by any State since the birth of Christ. Nero's persecution was because of religion; so with Spain in expelling the Moors and Jews; and so with the massacre of the Hugenots by Charles IX of France in the sixteenth century; so, too, the slaying of Mexicans and Peruvians by Cortez and Pizarro, incited an excess of miscalled religious zeal, which is being exemplified by Christian nations in China. But we of America were of the same history, religion and lineage and believed alike in constitutional government. Hence that cruel law was without the shadow of excuse and many well informed men think that its enactment caused more deaths than either of the persecutions mentioned. It has been truthfully said that civilization is but a veneer. Had conditions been reversed, the South would probably have enacted the same laws. Let us be thankful for the unlooked for result, a free and united country.

This bitter subject recalls a pleasant reminiscence; memory of things long past, which, like distance, lends enchantment. That indeed is an ill wind that blows no one good, and I profited by that mean law. H. G. Hendricks and myself attended the first session of the District Court held in Johnson County after the war. Buchanan was then the county seat, situated away from water, on the high prairie, twenty-six miles due south of Fort Worth on the old military road between Fort Worth and Fort Graham on the Brazos. There is no town there now, for Cleburne has absorbed it. The Johnson County Court was important. That county then embraced Hood, Somervell and a part of Ellis Counties. The officers were —— Scott, Judge (appointee) ; James Hiner, Clerk, and Joseph Shaw, Sheriff.

A party kept the saloon, a brand new one, built of post oak logs, about twelve feet square and covered with oak boards. It had a loft, approached by a ladder. His stock in trade was one barrel of New Dexter. You could smell the oak timbers on entering, which I did, on business bent. Saturday came and our court was about to adjourn. I had defended the party who owned the saloon in several small cases and in one serious one. He had paid the fees in the misdemeanor cases with stock in trade, but concerning the larger fee, he told me, in a mysterious way, that he was out of money, but had a quantity of French quinine, which he had "confiscated" at Tyler, where he was guard in the Confederate army at the wind-up; that owing to the Uncle Jimmy Gathan and other troubles, he was afraid to keep it, and had it in a trunk upstairs. Now, I had refused, on the advice of Jacob Samuels, my merchant, to appropriate some thirty bales of Confederate wool, which I found stored in one end of my office in Fort Worth, and which Uncle Isaac Duke Parker took in the name of the United States. This wool was worth 50 cents a pound, and was actually in my possession, and I regretted not having confiscated it. So, profiting by my experience, I told my client I would take the drug and credit it as far as it would go. Getting my saddlebags and my black-dyed Yankee overcoat, up the ladder we went, and from an old hair trunk filled the saddlebags and overcoat pockets with genuine French quinine in big-mouthed ounce bottles, tying my clothing behind the saddle a la valise in returning home. In those days, Texas being a dryer country than now, an almost universal custom prevailed of stopping to take a drink just before crossing running water. It was considered bad luck to do otherwise; and the custom was venerable by age and sanctioned by public opinion. So Hendricks and myself, observing this custom, stopped at the bank of Nolan River, where I surprised him with a gift of part of the royal fee.

Mr. Samuel J. Darcey, a wounded veteran, then kept our village drug store. He disposed of my fee at retail at $16 an ounce, the whole amounting to several hundred dollars. At the ensuing term of court, no witnesses appearing against my client, he went hence without day.

PATRIOTISM IN THE SCHOOLS.

It is just one measured mile on Main street in Fort Worth from the center of the Union depot to the center of the courthouse—two of the finest buildings in the Southern States—inspiring one at a glance with the volume of ideas contained in those three words—wisdom, strength and beauty. Both of these no less useful than magnificent buildings are furnished with flagstaffs. How beautiful on clear days to see our flag flying from these buildings! The cost would be so light, the effect so glorious!

When Henry C. Holloway was County Commissioner the county owned a splendid flag. Commissioner Barr tells me that it is worn out. Then buy another, or several if advisable, and see to it that the Sheriff does his duty at the halyards. I know he will, for the law would compel him, if so ordered by your County Commissioners.

The nation at large has at last learned that we old Confederates long ago furled the flag we loved, and that we have taught and teach our children to venerate and love the flag of our fathers. In England the war of the roses, between the Houses of York and Lancaster, lasted for nearly two generations. It left England a united people, as is America today.

The flag is the emblem of patriotism, and a nation without patriotism is liable to destruction at any time. We have several large public school buildings besides the High School building, each with its ever-naked, lonesome, solemn, yet inviting flagstaff. It is more important that the children be taught patriotism at school than any other study, and in this the national flag is the object lesson. Make manning the colors each weak an honorable office to be coveted by male students. Our law properly prohibits the teaching of religion in the schools. But patriotism? The schools should be the hotbeds of patriotic inspirations, symbolized by the flag of our fathers.

SHALL THE WHIPPING POST BE REVIVED?

Texas, separated from older nationalities, evolved written and economic laws peculiar to herself and enforced by local necessities.

Punishment in the Orient by the bastinado and in Russia by the knout, suits their conditions, for jails, penitentiaries and reform schools do not exist in the deserts of Arabia, or on the steppes of Russia.

So, too, in religious beliefs human races differ as widely as people differ from one another, because they are mentally moulded that way, and logically evolve religious beliefs accordingly.

English speaking people from the time of King John have always and everywhere successfully contended for trials by jury. Sometimes, however, owing to lack of prisons punishment was prematurely inflicted before the court passed final judgment.

A Case in Point.

Some years before the Civil War, when this country was almost a wilderness, and when there was no town of Denton in Texas, District Court was held in a place called Old Alton, in Denton County. John C. McCoy, of Kentucky, was prosecuting attorney, and Gustavus Adolphus Everetts, of Illinois, was attorney for the defendant. Charge, theft of a saddle. The jury found the defendant guilty. Everetts immediately filed a motion for new trial, whereupon court adjourned for dinner. Resuming labor, Everetts presented his motion, backed by an able argument, during which now and then the defendant interrupted by pulling at his coat tail and finally said: "Stop it; they'll whip me again." During recess the Sheriff had anticipated final judgment by inflicting the punishment.

How He Got Even.

When the county site was finally located at Denton, Everetts got even with Mac, who was prosecuting a man for assault and battery, Everetts again defending. From the jury box could plainly be seen the large new sign of "Restaurant," where the fight occurred. It was about an evenly balanced case. Mac made a strong speech and properly pronounced the word "restauraw." Concluding for the defence, Everetts said: "My learned friend who lives in ̠alias close to Frenchtown, and who speaks that language, is as much in error as to the law and facts of this case as he is in pronouncing the word "restaurant." Now, gentlement (pointing to the sign), please spell that word with me. R-e-s; don't that spell res? T-a-u; don't that spell rester? R-a-n-t; don't that spell restaurant? And if it don't spell restaurant, in the name of goodness what do it spell? Of course the defendant went hence without day.

Whipped and Cleared.

Hicks says that his father lived on the side of a sandy hill in North Carolina. One day a man indicted for petty larceny was seen slowly wending his way up hill with dejected mien, and being asked whither he was going, he solemnly replied: "To the courthouse to stand my trial." In the evening this man reappeared and when asked as to how his trial came out, with body erect and head thrown back, he replied. "They whipped me and cleared me; I'm all right!"

Now, this was better for the taxpayers and for the defendant and his family than a fine or an idle time in jail.

Shall we not revive the whipping post in Texas? It works well in one or two Northern States.

JACOB SAMUEL AND LEE CHALMERS.

The appearance in our city of the Hon. Lee Chalmers, Assistant Attorney General of the United States, recalls an incident in which Mr. Chalmers, Mr. Jacob Samuel, of this city, and myself, figured. We were bachelors then. Chalmers was an Austin boy, on the staff, and the very prince of good fellows. Until the winter of 1864 Waller's Batallion and Greene's Brigade had been on the move, and until we came to anchor at Virginia Point, near Galveston, we had experienced little suffering from want of fire-heat. Here in midwinter, on this bleak, barren sand beach, with poor water and miserable rations, with but three green pine sticks a day to the mess, without tents, in damp, cold weather, we had rather a hard time. I obtained permission to spend two days in the city of Galveston, with one man. I took with me Mr. Samuels. Lee Chalmers was also off duty, and we three took in the town together, Sam and I on virtue bent, for the purpose of visiting the Masonic lodge. We were accosted on the street by a bevy of beautiful girls, who importuned us to buy tickets to a lottery drawing for the benefit of war widows and orphans. Now, I had ever held conscientious scruples against engaging in raffles and gambling generally, even to assist church festivals, and so informed my companions and the insistent ladies; but Mr. Samuels said if the dice were all right the law of gravitation would make the result, which would be providential. Not daring to fly in the face of Providence, as it were, I reluctantly and with many misgivings consented and bought several tickets. Several of the prizes were valuable, and that night as the numbers of the tickets were called, the owners of the numbers advanced and threw for themselves. I got the presiding houri—the prettiest girl on any island— to throw for me, and won a gold chain and locket and two gold bracelets; gave her the locket and chain, she gracefully bending her neck while I encircled it with the chain in my arms amid the plaudits of all. The bracelets I carelessly put in the hind pocket of my coat. Of course we became popular. Now in elections I abhor repeating, and no good Democrat will nor indeed can he now repeat; but there are times—well, that night Mr. Samuels slept soundly on the top of a cistern in the back yard, "While not a wave of trouble rolled across his peaceful breast." My Colonel, Ed Waller, and myself, were alike surprised next morning to find ourselves in the same bed. Sam and myself drew ourselves together early in the morning, and on taking a careful inventory found ourselves strapped and "enhungered." Finally Sam found the bracelets in my pocket, badly mashed, and with them rapidly disappeared 'round the corner to an "uncle." Tres bolas de ora. And in a few minutes he returned with a hatful of Coonfederate money, with the aid of which we three spent two days "in riots most uncouth, and vexed with mirth the drowsy ear of night." It was an oasis in the desert of our existence, soon followed by the march; then Mansfield, Pleasant Hill and Brashear City, where General Banks so liberally replenished our quartermaster and commissary stores.

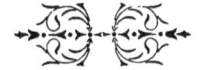

CONFEDERATE REUNION IN MEMPHIS.

The late reunion at Memphis was a success in every way. Mr. Andrew J. Harris, a kinsman of our historian, Judge C. C. Cummings, and whose palatial residence is three miles from the heart of the city, entertained General Van Zandt's staff with royal hospitality. Miss Maggie Cummings and Miss Lively, her maid of honor, of Bowie, Texas, were of the party. What with the hearty welcome, good cheer and music, we had a grand old time. The ancestral Cummings home, extensive lawn, large magnolia trees in full bloom, beautiful rose gardens, and esthetic taste everywhere, unostentatiously displayed, suggested the Old South.

I gladly accepted Mr. Harris' hospitality for the night. A member of the staff, our General Joe Wheeler (Colonel George Jackson), shared his bed with me. We were travel-worn, and after a large night-cap, slept soundly. "Not a wave of trouble rolled across our peaceful breast." It was rainy and chilly without, but an old-fashioned coal fire, music and mirth, made all bright and genial within.

After awhile the young people suggested tales of war time, and when the ante was passed to me I told the following reminiscence:

At the commencement of the Civil War the Confederate government confiscated the Northern enemy's property for the use of the Confederacy; for instance, the firm of Turner & Daggett, in Fort Worth, were indebted in New York for $30,000 for goods. The firm paid that sum to the Confederacy, and after the war paid off their New York creditors also. United States District Judge Duval, being a Union man, was, by order of President Davis, superseded by Thomas J. Devine of San Antonio. Judge Devine appointed me Confederate receiver of public money and properties for my portion of the state. Experience having taught me that it was more blessed to receive than to give, I gladly accepted the position, and obeying instructions, reported in person with bond, etc., to the court at San Antonio.

The State Constitutional Convention had submitted to the people the question: Shall Texas secede from the Federal compact? At this time it was not a question of peace or war, for some Southern States had seceded and war was inevitable. Governor (then Doctor) Throckmorton, Governor Sam Houston, and M. P. Johnson, C. Caldwell, John Peter Smith, D. C. Dade and myself, among others of Tarrant County, favored separate action for Texas and opposed the raising of a new flag. We were pretty evenly divided; Tarrant County voted for secession by a majority of only 28 out of over 700 votes cast.

Returning from San Antonio, I visited old friends on the Mountain in Hill County, Louis Hutchison and his wife (nee Miss Laura Lawton); they were highly educated and wealthy, and had no children, had been to Cuba and elsewhere in search of health; lived—or rather, camped—in a one-room little log cabin in a beautiful grove near a fine spring and in the midst of an apparently boundless prairie, miles distant from the nearest neighbor and just dimly in sight of the Cross Timbers to the west. Louis and Miss Laura had found here in this quasi-wilderness what they had sought in vain, robust health. They were in love with each other and with their surroundings. They had a wagon, horses, a few cows and calves, and a glorious little garden. They told me they had no wish unsatisfied; were all in all to each other. I never met so happy a young couple. They were devoted members of the Baptist church. Louis had, like myself, been educated at the Kemper school, in Boonville, Mo. He was a stranger to Lord Bacon's philosophy, had never read Huxley, Darwin or Proctor, and only heard adversely of Tom Payne and Voltaire, and of the doubts of the Adamses, Thomas Jefferson and Benjamin Franklin on the Scriptures. He possessed the unbounded faith of a little child approaching the mustard-seed variety; he gave undoubted credence to the whale, bear, serpent tale, and all. Alas, the direful rumors of approaching Civil War had reached this isolated, happy couple, and clouded their lives. Conservative people were slow to express themselves politically, and I was at a loss to know where to place Louis until bedtime, when, after reading a chapter in the Bible, where Joshua commanded the sun to stand still and Moses had his hands held up, he reverently knelt at the old trunk and there, oblivious of surroundings, unburdened his pure heart and told his soul's sincere desire which he had in a measure withheld from me. He said: "If the North is right in interfering with our domestic institutions, . . . contrary to the Federal Constitution and against the solemn decision of the Supreme Court, then O Lord, help thou the North; but, but, and if, O thou God of heaven and earth, the South is right (and we believe in our hearts that she is) in defending her property peacefully and legally acquired and held, then, O Lord, smite thou the Northern robbers hip and thigh from the rising to the going down of the sun even to the dividing apart of bone and marrow." I no longer doubted Louis's soundness.

They on account of the war returned to Missouri, and there in that rough climate, succumbed to the terrible disease, as much victims of the war as was Uriah, the victim of David the Anointed, the history of whose vile life, by the way, should be eliminated from our Sunday school and only found on the theological shelf of Carnegie's library.

BROTHER DEHART'S POWERFUL PRAYER.

As a general rule it is sinful to laugh at Divine services, but there are exceptions to all rules. Burns tells us that "an atheist's laugh is a poor exchange for Deity offended." Amusing incidents sometimes occur in moments and surroundings of great seriousness, and well balanced men and women have been seen to laugh and weep at the same time. Shakespeare mixes the farce in all his tragedies; and even Solomon, divinely accredited with 700 wives and 300 concubines, descends to the ridiculously humorous. Of all animal creation man alone laughs. We are told that there is a time to laugh, but sometimes we are tempted to laugh when we should weep. The intent constitutes the sin. With good intentions, but at fearful risk of offending the "cloth," I would recall an amusing incident.

Our section, defeated in the unequal encounter of arms, exploited by carpetbag government, something like our "colonies" now feel, our school funds robbed, with practical negro political domination, a stoical feeling of deepest gloom overspread the land, and culminated in religious meetings largely attended even in sparsely settled sections.

In 1866 I attended the first Court of Reconstruction period held in Wise County, then a part of the Sixteenth Judicial District. Judge Waddell of Grayson presided, Em Hawkins of Ellis, District Attorney. Dr. J. W. Throckmorton (afterwards Governor) of Collin County, Joe Carroll (afterwards Judge) of Denton County, and G. A. Everetts, H. G. Hendricks of Tarrant County, were among the "visiting bar." We arrived in Decatur the Saturday evening before court. Brother Shaw, a man of deep piety, of ripe age, and presiding elder of the Methodist Episcopal Church, South, was holding a prosperous camp meeting some four miles from town, and on Sunday night we all attended divine service there on pleasure and business bent, for a while some of us were piously inclined, all were impecunious, and the litigants were at the meeting. The moon was full, the weather fine.

There was present old Brother Dehart, a wealthy cattle owner, who was possessed of an article of spasmodic and intermittent religion then prevailing; for awhile he rejoined the church and prayed in public in summer; he fell off and got cold in winter. He was small of stature and was the only cattleman in Texas who wore a plug hat. He possessed an unusually loud, deep, musical voice, in volume equal to that of Mohamet's crier. He was not for prophecy or exhortation. He was powerful in prayer. Indeed, it was his religious specialty—public prayer. Dehart was noted for using melliflous and sometimes unmeaning words; so that they had the bigness and sound it was all right with him. For instance, petroleum was advertised in the paper, but unknown to many. It had been developing during the war. We had just learned of its great value, and of the millions made by its owners. During the height of the excitement caused by the elder's eloquent description of what G. W. Paschal in the introduction to his annotated digest called "an old-fashioned Methodist hell," Brother Dehart was called upon to pray. On the way to town we tried to remember that prayer. I remember the beginning and conclusion only. It ran something like this:

"O, thou all-sufficient, inefficient, self-sufficient being, O, thou almighty, all-powerful, omnipotent, omniscient, omnipresent, eternal, petroleum, insignificant, Lord Jesus H. Christ—eh—Jehovah God—eh—" and the conclusion, after a long breath—"And O, Lord—eh—when thou art tired and done serving thyself with us on earth—eh—wilt thou take us into that upper and better kingdom, prepared—eh— from the foundation of the earth, for the devil and his angels!"

Several cried, "God grant it!" but Brother Shaw exclaimed, "God Almighty, forbid!"

An alarm of Indians being in the country broke up the meeting the very next day. All above named have passed in their checks, and like Elijah, "I, even I only, am left." My attorney, and some time mentor, tells me that our offense of laughing then was only a venal sin, a sort of misdemeanor, and that he can beat it for me by pleading the statute of limitations, and Hyde knows.

"UNCLE" JACK DURRETT,
The Fiddler.

THE CHARMS OF MUSIC.

Fiddlers' Contest Evokes Memories of an Old Time Fiddler of Fort Worth.

The idea of having in Fort Worth a fiddlers' prize contest for the benefit of R. E. Lee Camp of Confederate Veterans is good and deserves success. All people have music in their souls, cultivated or dormant. The love of concord of sweet sounds is planted in the natures of lower animals as well. Music, with all people, is connected with ideas of the immortality of the soul. From the Indian's death song to the gorgeous notes of St. Peter's, music has ever been the assistant of religion. The Chinaman, enchanted with his weird music, is oblivious to the charms of Norma and Somnambula. His music and his religion suit him, and he should be left unmolested in their enjoyment. Music is enjoyed very largely by association, and very many, like myself, enjoy "Dixie," "Arkansaw Traveler," "Coming Thro' the Rye," "Annie Laurie," "Home, Sweet Home," "My Country, 'Tis of Thee," and pieces like those, more than we do the average music of Mendelssohn or Mozart. The gift of genius that can compose a hymn and music like "Jesus, Lover of my Soul," is more to be desired than the wealth of a Rockefeller.

The powerful effect of music on the emotional nature of man is shown in the following reminiscence:

In 1858, Uncle Jack Durrett came from Tennessee to Fort Worth, an aged man, of courtly bearing, who had inherited and spent two fortunes. Like Old King Cole, he was a jolly old soul, and a good fiddler. Then the eight-hour labor demand was unheard of, except by *Masons*. Business as such was only known in the cattle branding and round-up time. One evening in May, when the boys were congregated, as usual, on the west side of the square, killing time and listening to Uncle Jack's music, all eyes were turned to behold a fine, middle-aged man, dressed in steel-mixed homespun and riding a thoroughbred. Dismount ing he loosened his girth and hitched to the rack. He was evidently a well-to-do stranger, probably a land buyer, Now Uncle Jack was in his happiest mood, keeping time with his foot, with his head thrown back, and oblivious to surroundings. Hearing the music, the stranger silently advanced and stood close to the performer, and when the tune was finished, with tears coursing down his face, and as if speaking to himself, he exclaimed, "Dilcy Hawkins! Jest to think of hearing Dilcy Hawkins played away from Tennessee, out here in Texas. Please play 'Dilcy' again, old gentleman!" Uncle Jack readily encored, the stranger directing to the crowd a dignified and kindly look, and slightly extending his hand towards the proprietor, remarked, as near as can be remembered: "Gentlemen, will you jine me?" Ever thereafter he bore the title of Colonel.

Uncle Jack accompanied the Colonel to Larrie Steele's tavern, telling him on the way about the county site contest between Fort Worth and Birdville (which cost the lives of several good men). Coley Johnson, Hen Durret and Kid Nance, kids with instinctive love for a fine horse, led the charger to Netherley's stable.

If the contestants do not equal Orpheus or even Uncle Jack, they will entertain by recalling halcyon days of 'Auld Lang Sine,' when life was full of sunny dreams.

*   *   *   *   *   *   *

Uncle Jack, the embodiment of dignified politeness and geniality, was a born talker, and talked well, too. He had a stereotyped memory and was long on details. Once started, interruptions might give him pause, but recovering the thread, he pushed right on to the goal, however distant. He loved to talk and to fish. He had been known to fish for two days in one spot without getting a bite.

After mounting his horse next morning, the stranger asked Uncle Jack to tell him the road to Weatherford. With a bow-and-expectorating preface, he told him that Weatherford was the county seat of Parker County, which was just thirty miles square and twenty-eight miles due west of Fort Worth; to leave R. H. and William King's blacksmith shop to the left, and also Fields' mill, where Judge

Seaborn Gilmore licked the miller who was charged with over-tolling; then to cross Clear Fork below the Blue Hole, where Parson A. N. Dean baptized C. A. Harper, and where Larry Steele's steers and negro were drowned; rising the bank on the other side he'd see a log cabin with a wagon road on both sides, where 'Squire Stephen Terry married a couple, who, ignoring their tents, and against advice, lodged over night in that empty, unchinked cabin, which leaked like a sieve—it thundered and rained all night, I don't think they slept much that night; do you?' The stranger gave a smiling assent—the horse became more restless—proceeding Uncle Jack told him to take either road, for they came together in 300 yards; proceeding due west he would leave the first house to his left; that Uncle John Kinder lived there, concededly the best off-hand rifle shot in Texas, though Judge Gilmore, C. G. Payne and Paul Tyler were good seconds—the horse and rider became more restless—seeing this Uncle John said, 'The fact is, stranger, there is but one plainly traveled road from here west, and it leads directly to Weatherford. Follow that road and leave Prince's mill and Dr. Blackwood's tavern to the left and you will land at Carson & Lewis's brick hotel.'

Raising his voice, as the stranger rode off, he said, 'Dr. Blackwell being from the State of Kentucky, you better stop with him.'

Capt. M. B. Loyd says that the stranger stopped with Mrs. Curtis, who afterwards married Mr. Cullom and then Mr. Sykes.

Uncle Jack straightened up, about faced and struck a bee line for Tom Prindle's saloon on the west side of the square.

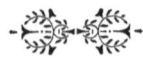

PECAN TIME IN BIRDVILLE.

Our constitution wisely provides that in all criminal prosecutions the accused shall be confronted with the witnesses against him.

In the days of reconstruction Birdville used the public school house for religious worship. Lon Barkley, a lad of about sixteen, with new red-top boots, pants inside, inclined to a different faith to Parson W., a very nervous spare made man, a local preacher.

The latter took Phillip and the eunuch for his text. It was pecan time, a heavy crop, and the floor was covered with hulls. Every time Mr. W. made a 'p'int,' down would come Lon's boot heels on the hulls, till W. Prematurely adjourned his meeting. Lon was indicted, charged with disturbing religious worship, and Rev. W. was State's witness.

"In the cross-examination I asked him to state to the court and jury his feelings toward the defendant. He said, with a pious sigh of resignation, looking toward the ceiling, "As for the lad, in the Spirit I do dearly love him, but" (looking sternly at the defendant, with uplifted arm and cleanched fist, and with a loud voice) "as for the lad in the flesh, I do hate, abominate and abhor him, so help me God.'

"Defendant was acquitted on the ground that Parson W. could not hold a religious meeting under the statutes.

"Lon —— yet says the other boys did it."

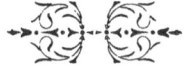

UNCLE JOHN KINDER, THE FAMOUS SHOT AND HUMANITARIAN.

It was in Fort Worth, the first day of the fall term of the District Court, in 1858. The grand jury had been empaneled and charged and the docket sounded. The term was limited to one week, which required day and night work, especially on the part of the clerk. A shooting match was on the tapis and many rifles were in sight. All hands, including the court and jurors, adjourned to the bottom at the junction of the Trinity Rivers where the power house stands, and where Uncle Charley Daggett had a ferry. Here an unbranded 7-year-old break-fence steer stood lariated to a young pecan tree. He was a beauty. Red-and-white pied, fat as mud, with horns stained red with poke-berries and, surrounded by the admiring crowd, who variously commented on the marksmanship of the contestants. The rule was fifty yards off-hand and seventy-five yards with a rest, at the option of the marksman.

Uncle John Kinder, who lived at the site of Arlington Heights, being the oldest man—in his sixties—was given the first shot. He was a pioneer from Illinois, over six feet tall, a kindly man, with cold, steel-gray eyes, and a Universalist in belief. He loved his rifle. She was long and heavy, maple-stocked and silver-mounted—carried thirty-two to the pound. Her hair-triggers (which Randolph abominated) were as sensitive as the mimosa. When Uncle John toed the mark all were silent and intense. Closely shaved, with head thrown back, he stood as straight as a pine, resting his body on his right leg, the left well extended; for only a moment he sighted. Firing, a shout went up from non-contestants. The center had been driven in. Uncle John had won. The hide and tallow also were his.

That he was a remarkable shot there is no doubt. An old settler tells this: "Long prior to 1857, when I came to Fort Worth, on a calm, clear, lazy spring day, when 'there was not a breeze on high the gossamer to bear,' several men and post officers were at the sutler's store. Uncle John was there with rifle in hand, as usual. A young officer guyed him about his marksmanship, and, pointing to a large buzzard, low-circling above, asked him to bring it down. He said: 'The buzzard is a useful bird, and to kill it would be against the law; but I will slightly wing him.' Firing, a small feather was slowly wafted to their feet, at which the bird, seeming unconcerned, wobbled a little. Slowly reloading, he remarked: 'Boys, I hate cruelty. Next time he circles I will trim him even,' and firing, behold! another feather from his left wing, with the bird flying off evenly. The feathers were of the same length."

Now, in those days when local option was undiscovered, and all whisky was good, it was in demand at house-raisings and general elections; but shooting matches, where keen eyes and steady nerves won, were the exceptions. So the crowd adjourned to the public square and Uncle John was the hero of the hour. Here he bet A. Y. Fowler, a young attorney, that he would shoot through, or merely hit a box without the bullet going through. Retiring to the back room of Oldham's store, he unscrewed the small end of his ramrod, and with tow taken from his fawn-skin hunting pouch, wiped out the gun, and with a buck-horn charger loaded with powder, slapped the lock, rolled a round unpatched bullet down the barrel and inserted a loose paper wad within one inch of the muzzle, primed, half-cocked and rejoined the crowd. With rifle to his face he asked Fowler to bet, which he did, and on the bullet going through. Whereupon Uncle John elevated the breech of his gun, causing the ball to roll down to the paper, and, firing, made a small dent on the box. The two gallons went the round, including the bench and the visiting bar, more than once. The court had a good send-off. He was a hospitable, sympathetic, sociable and neighborly man.

"The Simple Annals of the Poor."

A few miles west of Fort Worth, in a little valley between Arlington Heights and Mrs. Henry Thompson's, during the Civil War, lived a poor, aged, one-eyed man, a plasterer from Missouri, named Malloy. He was a preemptor under the law of '56.

His household consisted of himself and two children, aged 5 and 7 years. Uncle John Kinder and Malloy were enemies, and, although neighbors, they had not spoken for months. Then wolves were numerous. One night Malloy fell sick and told the children that in the morning he would be dead, and that they must on account of the wolves stay in the cabin until sun-up, and then go and tell Uncle John to bury papa. Uncle John complied with the request and cared for the little ones.

LEWIS H. BROWN FAMILY.

Looking over the "Puritan" for August I was struck with the familiarity of the face and figure of Countess Adam Von Moltke-Huitfeldt (formerly Miss Bonaparte, of Washington.)

There was a something in the likeness which at once suggested that I had seen or that I was acquainted with the original.

In 1857, Lewis H. Brown came to Fort Worth from Maryland, near the city of Baltimore. His wife and five children came with him. Misses Lou and Ruth, pretty and accomplished young women, and Horatio, George and Harry, boys of honor and integrity. I think they are all dead now.

Mrs. Lewis Brown was a sister to Mrs. Jerome Bonaparte, the sister-in-law of the great Napoleon, and her above named children were cousins of the Countess, whose picture in the "Puritan" arrested my attention.

Horatio Brown was a member of my company in the Confederate army. I know the family intimately and hence my recognition of the family resemblance between the Countess and her whilom Texas kindred.

The "Puritan" article reads:

An American Countess.

"Scarcely a season passes without a marriage between some Washington belle and a member of one of the foreign legations at the American capital. One of the latest acquisitions of the diplomatic corps is the Countess Adam Von Moltke-Huitfeldt, nee Bonaparte, whose maiden name suggests a historical international romance. She is the great granddaughter of the Miss Elizabeth Patterson, of Baltimore, who became the wife—the legal, though discarded wife—of Jerome Bonaparte, King of Westphalia, and brother of the great Napoleon. On the side of her mother, who was Miss Caroline Leroy Appleton, she is a great granddaughter of Daniel Webster. The Empress Eugenie was her godmother."

SANTA ANNA'S SILVER WASH BASIN.

There is inate in the human mind a regard for relics and curios carried by some even to the extent of quasi worship.

Do I believe in encouraging such regard? I do, when the end favors altruism or patriotism.

Just after the war with Mexico, I remember when traveling on the Mississippi River below St. Louis, all the passengers went on deck to get a better view of "Old Whitie," General Zachary Taylor's war horse grazing in a pasture.

What kid visits the National Capital without a sight of General Washington's well-worn clothes and his camp utensils used at Valley Forge and the wall papering at Mount Vernon done by General La Fayette's own hands.

But right here in Tarrant County Mrs. Josephine Ryan, the step-granddaughter of Capt. E. M. Daggett, owns the silver *wash basin* captured from General Santa Anna by Daggett in the Mexican War in 1847. Captain Daggett commanded a cavalry company in the famous Jack Hays Texas Regiment at the time. In 1857, General Houston and Hardin R. Runnels were candidates for Governor of Texas. Runnels was the nominee of the Democratic Waco Convention, of which Daggett was a member, while Houston ran independently. General Houston and Lewis T. Wigfall—who spoke in behalf of Runnels—met in discussion at Birdville in this county, but passed the night in Fort Worth. Runnels accepted the hospitality of Col. Nat Terry while Capt. Daggett entertained General Houston. Houston's wound in the leg, received in the battle of San Jacinto in 1836, was a running sore, and in fact never healed. It needed frequent dressing, and Captain Dagget used this Santa Anna silver wash bowl that night, and with his own hands dressed the wound. Nevertheless Captain Daggett voted for Runnels, although he was a dear lover of Houston. General Houston was not then forgiven by the people of Texas for presenting to the United States Senate the "petition of ten thousand vice-regents of Heaven (preachers) for the abolition of slavery in the District of Columbia and in the ports, arsenals and dock yards of the United States."

Surely, this relic, hallowed by such memories should be deposited in our Carnegie Library with the curios presented by Capt. M. B. Loyd, Judge A. W. Terrell and other donors, to be seen of all.

True, we have the face of Captain Daggett on our city seal, but his name could better be perpetuated by presenting this historical relic as indicated.

OVERLAND TRIP TO CALIFORNIA IN '52 WITH EXTRACTS FROM MY OLD DIARY.

My wife placed in my hands an old book containing memoranda of my overland trip to California in 1852, and asked me to write an account of that journey.

I was raised on a farm near Booneville, Mo., and was educated there at Kemper school. Of course most of my associates were frontier boys. All could swim, and most of them were good shots. I had read Lewis & Clark's book, Cooper's novels, and Irving's works, but longed to see the Great West for myself. Two years I had lived in St. Joseph, Mo., with my brother and guardian, A. W. Terrell.

At this point most of the California, Salt Lake, and Oregon emigrants bought their outfit, a matter of great importance for a journey of sixteen hundred miles through a wilderness, where neither love nor money could procure the necessaries of life. My company was composed of three: A. Fuqua, a widower, farmer, 35 years old; Powhatan B. Whitehead, a cowboy, 23, and myself, 20 years old. I owned most of the outfit. Our wagon was well covered and had sideboards extending over the wheels, affording room for sleeping in rainy weather, but ordinarily we preferred sleeping on the ground. We had three yoke of oxen, one yoke of milch cows, a good dog—Ranger—a few extra yoke bows, some small rope, two horses, some extra horseshoes and nails, axe, hatchet, auger and a few other things in that line in the tool box. As for medicines, five gallons of pure cognac brandy, some Tutt's pills and a few bottles of lemon syrup and acetic acid to counteract alkali water, constituted our dispensary.

Thinking the trip to Sacramento City could be made in four months, provisions were laid in accordingly, consisting of flour in sacks, prepared corn meal, dried fruit, rice, beans, coffee, tea, bacon, etc. We had a tray, an oven, two frying pans, skillet and coffee pots, two water buckets, a lantern, candles, tin plates, cups, matches, etc. Of course we had good arms and ammunition, a plentiful supply of fishing tackle, and a good tent. The latter proved to be a nuisance, and in three weeks we threw it away, retaining the fly.

On the 3rd day of May, 1852, I started from St. Joseph, Mo., and camped four miles above the city, at Duncan's Ferry. Under a written contract with my partners I was to neither cook, drive nor milk, but was to care for my own horse and stand guard only. This was like written republican constitutions to the Latin races—good in theory but bad in practice. I could yoke up and drive oxen, but could not milk. However, there was work enough for all, and we got on well to the last, except as to the milking. My partners loved coffee. The cows were soon dried up, and I substituted sugar and water for milk.

I always hated to tell my friends good-bye. The weather was gloomy, cold, and rainy, and I, drenched to the skin, slept in my clothes the first night in camp. My only relative in Missouri had moved to Austin, Texas, and, raised an orphan, unused to labor or hardship of any kind, I felt for the first time practically alone in the world and dependent solely upon myself.

Next day we crossed the Missouri river in a flat boat. Passing through what is now Doniphan County, Kansas, a most beautiful country, some twenty-five miles to the Indian agency, dined with Major Richardson, the agent, and he, with his family, bade me God speed. "Drs. Beckham and Taylor are waiting here for Perry's train to take them to California." So even then passenegers were taken across, fed, etc., by contract, but never, so far as I know, with satisfaction to the passengers.

The Wells family, also of St. Joseph, consisting of the aged couple and six children—five boys and one girl—the youngest, Miss Cassie, 18 years old, graduate of a New York seminary, and highly accomplished. She sang and played well on the guitar. The five brothers were illiterate, but stout, brave, good men, hunters and trappers, and for years had, with their guns and traps, supported their parents and educated Miss Cassie, the idol of the family. Their outfit consisted of two large wagons loaded with all sorts of provisions and absolutely all of their homestead furniture, from old bedsteads to the family clock. They even brought the chickens along, and they were trained so as to give little trouble. Mrs. Wells said she left only the ash hopper. Their teams were oxen and cows, and they had several fine riding horses and some loose cattle. Miss Cassie's four-year-old baby gelding was a beauty, but looked sie's four-year-old bay gelding was a beauty. Cassie's complexion was very fine, her hair long and black, and often worn "a la Indian." Her eyes were coal black. She stood a little over the medium height; in form a very Venus. She loved books. I had brought some along, mostly romances, and when the weather was good we would ride several miles ahead of the train to pick the camping ground, and with books and fishing tackle whiled away the time until our folks came up. We thus traveled many a hundred miles, to Independent Rock, on Weber River, in now Wyoming Territory. A red-headed man from Pike County, Illinois, was working his way across with the Wells. He was very partial to Miss Cassie, always attended to her horse, and expressed unusual concern as to her safety when with me. Of course I became suspicious. From the 8th to the 15th nothing of interest transpired except an occasional stampede and the many deaths from Asiatic cholera and smallpox. Dr. Beckham says that he attributes the numerous deaths to self-administration of strong remedies, coupled with unaccustomed exposure. I am glad we brought only the pills and brandy, yet untaken and untasted. Mrs. Dawson, a friend from St. Jo., an elderly widow lady, died today of cholera. She was accompanied by two grown daughters and was their only protector. Their brother, John, is a wealthy man, a "49er" and proprietor of the Dawson House in Sacramento City.

The officials at Fort Kearney estimated that over 31,000 people, of both sexes and all ages, passed overland this year. The number that died can never be known. I saw hundreds of newly-made graves. In some instances the remains were buried so shallow that they were scratched up and devoured by wolves, the torn shrouds and bones being all that was left. Seeing this, some would haul rocks from a distance to place on the graves of their dead, and thus baffle the wolves. This country was infested by a large gray wolf, as big as the Texas "loafer" wolf. They were more numerous near large herds of buffalo, and preyed upon the aged, young and diseased of these beasts.

As a rule the emigrants honored the Sabbath day and tried to keep it holy by laying over. Sometimes we listened to sermons from divines of various beliefs. We were often regaled by good music, songs in different languages, and we had an occasional dance.

The herding and guarding of the stock was of vital importance, and they were closely guarded at night. This caused great loss of sleep, and I, like Joseph in Pickwick Papers, was young and sleepy-headed. I more than once, in after years, shielded boy soldiers from punishment for being caught napping on guard duty. Every night from two to three hours guard duty. It was horrible!

How, in such a multitude, far removed from civilization, without officers or jails, were the vicious restrained and punished and the weak and good protected? Judge Lynch presided; a rough tribunal, from whose judgments there was no appeal. Hung juries and new trials were unknown. His decisions were universally applauded—or criticised with rare discretion. To illustrate: One morning, cooking breakfast, two partners quarreled. One, stooping over a skillet, was, from behind, stabbed to the heart. His slayer was immediately disarmed and his hands tied. A man had presided as Judge in Illinois, a stranger, was forced to preside as Judge, and attorneys appointed to prosecute and defend; a jury of twelve men, also strangers, were empaneled; and, after argument and charge, the defendant was found guilty and sentenced to be hung—which was done instanter, from two elevated wagon tongues tied together, the forewheels scotched with ox-yokes, for there were neither trees nor rocks. The foregoing, set out in legal parlance and signed by the judge and jury and tacked to a board, was placed on the grave.

We had been traveling in a northwesterly direction from St. Jo. "The country is a wilderness, abounding in game; it is very windy and cold," says my old diary. Right here I remember being on guard twice in one night. I made oxen get up that I might lie down and benefit from their warm places. Neither Fuqua nor Whitehead were good cooks. Anything that was filling would do them, while I, stout as a bullock, was rather fastidious. We had been living on plain flapjacks, bacon and coffee. The cows were about dried up. My desire for variety was laughed at by the others, and although we had lots to eat in our stores, dried fruit, etc., they would not cook it for me, and I did not know how to cook it. I told them that to do my guard duty that night I would kill an antelope —numbers being in sight—so about 3 o'clock I pitched out about a mile from camp and hid in a gully, and by putting my hat on my ramrod and raising and lowering it, brought them within fifty yards. I brought down a fat buck and packed his hams to camp. Pow went for the remainder and only returned with part. The ever watchful wolves got the rest. Who would think that ambition, away out here in the wilderness, would exist? I copy from my journal: "We would have had quite a pleasant time but for the disposition of some to push themselves forward as captains and commanders." Met Mr. Joseph Rheohadeux, of St. Jo. He had counted 3,500 wagons between this and Fort Laramie.

24th of May: Am troubled with great boil on my neck. Arrived at the Main Platte, which gives its turbid appearance to the Missouri. Had a good bath, and waded across to Grand Island, in water only two feet deep. Arrived at Fort Kearney. The commander told me that he would not furnish government provisions to those going west, but would give provisions to those discouraged and wishing to return to the States. He furnished me the following:

"Going West to Date—8,174 men, 1,286 women, 1,776 children, 2,543 horses, 2,316 mules, 26,269 cattle, 264 wagons, 501 sheep, and one hog."

So we were just in the rear of one-third of the total westward emigration for the year. This from the journal:

"Twelve miles above Fort Kearney, at the junction of the roads, we held a council and unanimously agreed to cross the river and take the Council Bluffs road."

Here the river is from one to two miles wide and from two to four feet deep, with quicksand bottom, and in crossing the wagon made a noice like the rolling of pork barrels. I waded over half way across, assiting the drivers. Camped half a mile below the ford, on second bottom; lifted the wagon bed with props above the running gear so as to keep provisions from getting wet. The flour sacks did get wet. I feared that it would spoil the flour, but an old trapper said, "This little bath will do it good; only the sacks are wet;" and he was right. Here we brought out the washboards and did general washing. It was my first experience, and I was not included in the "contract." Some beautiful mountain streams flow south into the Platte, and one day Miss Cassie and I, going up stream to find a spring, on turning a hill came within 300 yards of a large Pawnee Indian camp. Halting, I told her to flee to the train, some three miles south of us, while I followed slowly, covering her retreat, until admonished by the proximity of the Indians and a shot from them, when I double-quicked and joined her in about 300 yards of our train. She saw the Indians, and heard the shooting; it was a nice little scare. The Indians did all in their power to herd the buffalo and other game from the trail. Feeling somewhat of a hero, I called on the Wells that night. Of course our being chased was the theme, and the speed of our horses alone saved us. The red-haired man's remarks were not complimentary. Fool that I was, I was too young then to understand. We would miss the Wells. Today we had a feast. Joe Wells killed a young elk and divided. But for Buffalo chips we would fare badly for fuel. "Pow" takes one side of an open two-bushel sack, and I, holding the other side, in a walk of a hundred yards, we filled it with old buffalo chips. It is best first to start a small wood fire, placing elk and deer horns above, to insure ventilation; then cover with chips, and in a short time you have a good fire. Wait a little, and from the horns and bones you have a lasting fire for boiling purposes.

Here we have the buffalo, the Indian's beef, furnishing robes and fuel. With the buffalo passes the wolf, which feeds upon them; then the beef steer appears; the bear, the Indian's bacon, lapses, and lo, the hog appears, for the white man—and the upbuilding of our *Fort Worth*.

Several hundred of the Mormons, from nearly every country in Europe, wintered in St. Jo. and en route to Salt Lake. Many small, two-wheeled carts are hauled by their young women, tandem, being loaded with children, etc. They get along about as well as we do. Young women stand hardship and exposure far better than men or their elders of either sex. They dance longer, with more vim, retire later and get up earlier than the opposite sex. I met quite a belle, a well educated Morman English lady, at a ball at the City Hotel in St. Jo., then kept by Major A. J. Vaughn. She loved to defend her church and boldly announced her belief in polygamy, and attributed the physical superiority of the Turks to their temperate lives and this plank in their religious platform. These people are good mechanics; some well educated; but all off color on the Bible question, and my study of them has caused me to be exceedingly charitable concerning their belief in the unknown and unknowable.

Col. A. W. Doniphan, who led the famous expedition through North Mexico in 1847, the hero of the battle of Sacramento, and who was instrumental in expelling the Mormons from Missouri, gave me a letter of introduction to Brigham Young. I wanted to go through Salt Lake City, but, although owner of the outfit, I had but one vote, and north of Salt Lake we went, about 100 miles. The Mormons having been roughly expelled from Illinois and Missouri, hated people from those States, therefor Illinois and Missouri emigrants, as a rule, took the northern route. That emigrants from these States were roughly handled by the Mormons there is no doubt. Even at that time, the Federal Judge had been expelled from Utah; the year following (1853) Col. Steptoe, of the Army, was appointed Governor in place of Brigham Young, removed, but Brigham said, "I am and will be Governor, and no power can hinder it until the Lord Almighty says, 'Brigham, you need not be Governor any longer;' " and he remained Governor.

This from my journal: "Came five miles to good camping ground; attempted to hunt game we saw on an island. We forded; I, being of low stature, led the way; Campbell, being tall, followed with ammunition and guns; he, less fortunate than I, fell in a deep hole and lost both. Determined to have our hunt out, we went several miles north of the trail, and, seeing ten objects which looked like buffalo, we approached and so did they. It was a Pawnee war party, without doubt, and at that time they were not friendly. They separated and tried to cut us off from the trail. We had the best horses, and, after a two-mile run they stopped. In a little bottom we ran at full speed through a prairie dog town, a dangerous thing to do, but we were excusable under the circumstances. Two of our company remained at a camp after we started, and following, passed ahead, we having turned out of the road to camp. They walked fully thirty miles before locating us, who had only come five miles. My dog's feet were worn sore by incessantly chasing game, especially mule-eared rabbits. I shod him with buckskin, tied on below his dew-claws, but finally made him ride in the wagon."

Here we are at Fort Laramie, a strong military position, situated at the junction and between the North and South Platte Rivers, the latter now mapped as Lawrence River, occupied by a strong garrison which raises its own corn and vegetables and attempts to hold down the finest looking and most warlike Indians on the continent, possessing numerous beautiful horses. Two years after this, in 1854, all this garrison, including women and children, were cruelly massacred by these Sioux Indians.

The oxen and horses must be shod—cows even worse than the oxen, pull against each other in the yoke, which wears off the outside of their hoofs. Changing them in the yoke does little good. "They charge here at the Government post private enterprise with a pull—sixteen dollars for shoeing oxen by the yoke, and fifty cents per dozen for nails. Having two good blacksmiths in our company, we paid twenty-five dollars for the use of the shop for one night. Our men made shoes, etc., from iron obtained from broken down vehicles. They made sixty-four shoes, with more nails than enough, and worked all night, thus saving $20.75. We surely thanked Mr. Campbell and Mr. Forman. Strange, I am too feeble to walk, yet feel that I am perfectly well. They falsely accuse me of taking a whole box of Tutt's pills, because the box was missing. Are traveling up north side of North Platte; hilly, dusty and very deep send; beautiful roses in sight, and general health of the voyagers good. Left the river; lots of blacktail deer.

23d June. Camped on Sweetwater River; with Miss Cassie ascended an elevation and obtained a most beautiful view of the surrounding country. One never tires of walking. We have arrived at Independence Rock. Right here Baron Von Humboldt camped, on the north side, and caused his name to be printed—the boys think with common tar —high up, but in a concave place, where rain can never reach. Walking this evening near camp I saw the name, in pencil, of my school chum, Ralph Douglass, of Bates County, Mo., on a cedar tree, the very last trace of him his family ever had.

I only mention the soda and hot springs left left behind. They exist in different countries; but Independent Rock, Echo Canon, and the Devil's Gate, to me, as curiosities of this continent rank with the Natural Bridge of Virginia and Niagara Falls. Arriving at the Devil's Gate we remained three days. Miss Cassie and I caught a string of small fish and loaded back to camp with cedar fagots. Made a trade with an Ohio man going to Oregon; swapped for his four splendid mules, in good condition, and gave him seventy-five dollars to boot and three yoke of oxen and two yoke of cows. The cows cost me forty dollars a yoke, and the steers seventy-five dollars a yoke, making the mules cost me about ninety-five dollars each. Opened a store and sold surplus provisions, clothing, etc., in opposition to Archambeaux, the trapper and trader, with Indian wife.

He has a store in twenty rods of us. How I hated to part from my animals and dog, all tried friends, for Ranger can not keep up with us now, going twenty to thirty-five miles a day. Swapped the wagon for pack saddles and some lessons on how to pack. I remember we placed the fat bacon, surrounded by flour. The principal difficulty was in learning to pack our molasses kegs. Now came trouble. It was agreed by us that each should take seven pounds of baggage and no more. I left lots of surplus clothing; gave Miss Cassie my books—of which I had quite a number—only retained a razor and strop, two pair of drawers and one strong hickory shirt. Only had one pair of well-worn moccasins, one pair of pants—buckskin—which have shrunk above my pastern joints. My straw hat is about worn out. This old weather-beaten journal in my lap, and the New Testament given me by my mother, are the only mementoes I retain of those days. We listened to a good sermon the night we arrived at the "Gate." I sat by Miss Cassie. We talked of parting, etc., until late at night. I passed her wagon; a candle was burning in it. Extending her arm from under the wagon seat she told me "Good-bye," and said, "I made this for you." That worn, sad, old book-mark, worked that night, over fifty years ago, is yet in the Testament. We had hunted and fished, climbed hills, read and "told tales" together for many weeks. It was real sad to part with Cassie, and, under the then conditions, I was just a little sorry for the red-haired man.

Poor Ranger, he followed us for two days, but finally had to give it up, for we made from twenty-five to thirty miles a day, and his feet could not stand it. I was tempted to shoot him. I bought a mare pony from Mr. Rheubadeau, of St. Jo., the very hardiest animal I ever saw, foaled in these mountains; she did not know grain, and kept fat—a natural pacer.

During the night the cayotes would attempt to steal our provisions, but we outwitted them by placing the provisions at our feet when we slept.

Every day we are passing those gentlemen who, in a urry, passed us. Generally their teams are poor and they

realize that they drove too hard. We are following Sweetwater River and are delighted with packing, now that we
are broken to adjusting the packs, etc. Camped on Little
Sandy, clear and deep, but fordable. Am troubled about
Mr. Fuqua's sickness, and neither "Pow" nor I know what
to do for him. He can hardly sit his mule, but is better
today. We are near perpetual snow. Heavy frost last night.
Slept cold beneath blankets. At the junction of the Fort
Hall and Salt Lake roads I took the latter twenty-five miles
so as to avoid Green River desert. Green River is a most
beautiful stream. Met my friend, J. Holliday, a Salt Lake
trader, and his assistant, C. H. Littler. Invited to dinner
by them. I was surprised. Eggs and new pork, new po-
tatoes and other vegetables, obtained in Salt Lake Valley
south of us; so, as this is the third, I count and celebrate it
for the Fourth of July, tomorrow being Sunday.

July 4, 1852. It snowed on us tonight, three and a half
inches. I was wet and cold all night, and in the morning
every bone in my body ached. The two days following I
was no better. They called it "mountain fever." It was
bilious fever.

One day, in looking across a deep depression to the top of
the opposite hill, some five miles, we saw the trail and
wagons there. The guide book said it would take thirty-five
miles travel to make that five miles. We decided to make
a short cut and boldly descended the hill, following what
seemed to be an old trail. We found the opposite ascent
too steep, and, going in a southwesterly direction for many
miles to a valley, we saw two Indians herding horses. Turning northward at the valley we were soon in a Sioux Indian village. The Indians assisted us in unpacking and
took our stock off, but did not disarm us. About dark they
set boiled meat before us, of which "Pow" and I ate hearti-
ly. Mr. Fuqua preferred jerked buffalo. The Indians returned our stock next morning. We in turn gave them
some ammunition, and with a general hand-shaking we
parted. Mr. Fuqua declared that "Pow" and I had eaten
stewed dog. He said he saw the head and hide of the dog,
and, as he never joked, we put it down as true.

Alkali dust is painful to eyes and lips in spite of goggles and veils, which are uncomfortably hot. Evidences of volcanic eruptions abound. It seems that every spot of the earth at some time has had its seismic troubles, and I know that water at one time covered all lands, because I saw beds of unmistakable oyster shells on the top of the Rocky Mountains.

On a hot day, fevered and jogging along on my mule, surrounded by clouds of alkali dust, I dreamed the same dream, or, rather, saw the same "vision" many times. I was comfortably seated in a large, cool hall with floor of tasselated marble, and ceiling supported by massive columns. From a distance a coal-black colored man, perspiring freely and wearing a snow-white cap and apron, holding with both hands a silver waiter, slowly approached. As he drew nearer I heard the tinkling sound of ice in a pitcher. He slowly filled a transparent goblet with water. I eagerly sized the vessel, whose coldness I could feel, and tremblingly placed it to my parched lips—here I awoke, so disappointed, to see Mr. Fuqua through the dust leading the mare pony followed by the pack mules and "Pow." This dream recalled Tentallus of old.

One day at noon, while Mr. Fuqua and "Pow" unpacked and made a fire, I took the bucket and went to a small mountain stream for water. Kneeling at the brink I saw a large mountain trout, near the grass-covered bank under me. I cut it in two with my side knife and secured the parts, started to camp with the water, and that is all I remember till awakened by "Pow," who said, "Come to dinner." The boil on my neck was immense in size and very painful. It had bursted, and they found me asleep in the sun on a big rock, the fish and water by my side. "Pow" had cooked the fish for me. Two days after this I shot a chaparal hen and "Pow" cooked that for me, too. He is a big-hearted man, and has learned to be a good cook. Weak and alseep I more than once fell off my mule. He made a wide circingle, with buckles to come over my knees, to strap, and thus tied me in the saddle. We were traveling then, according to the guide book, at the rate of twenty-five to forty miles a day. "Pow" never got sick, for he had lived an outdoor life. Poor fellow, I never saw him after we separated at Diamond Springs. He and Mr. Fuqua died within three years after crossing. We made a great mistake in parting with the wagon and its hundreds of comforts. Although slow, it was sure. The Wells were six months en route, but they came through healthy, with their stock in fine condition, when beef steak was worth fifty cents a pound. We had such confidence in our stock that we only hoppled one at a time and stood no guard. One night, camped near a willow thicket on a river, the stock came, frightened, to the very camp fire, caused by prowling Digger Indians, the lowest beings in the scale of humanity without a doubt. They would, from the willows, shoot arrows into cattle, which, killed or disabled, became their prey.

One day I overhauled one of these Indians and his wife. They had a worn-out emigrant pony, an old musket, the carcass of a freshly killed antelope strapped on the pony. I swapped a box of percussion caps and a little powder for half of the antelope, for which I was blamed by the older emigrants. We three, away off by ourselves, often tackled great questions. I remember that night, this trade with the Indian called up the question of the common descent of all men from Adam and Eve. "Pow" and I denied. Mr. Fuqua, a Presyterian, affirmed.

There is a great comfort in so simple a thing as a canteen. Mine was first covered with several layers of woolen goods, then with hog leather. Saturated and filled at night, by evaporation I had cool water all day, even when it was exposed to the sun.

The legs of my buckskin pants, once too long, have shrunken till they are six inches too short, and so are my drawers. Going west all the time, the heat of the sun has blistered my left leg. I prevent this by tying a sage bush to my knee. I have no socks, and the moccasins are about gone. Every clear, warm day, is wash day, at the noon rest, when we washed and waited for the garments to dı

At this high elevation the atmosphere is very rare, and

the explosion of a gun can be heard only a few rods. At the Devil's Gate, where we commenced packing, Archambeau gave us twelve pounds of yellow buffalo tallow for shortening bread and making gravy, a good change from pure bacon grease, and no bad substitute for butter.

At the South Pass in the Rocky Mountains there is a swamp, covering an acre of ground and abounding in springs, flowing east and west, into both oceans. "Pow" and I rode to the center and drank to the oceans.

A thousand details like these, which are not recorded, are vividly recalled by reading the journal. Provisions being lighter, I sold the weakest horse to a man traveling slow. Wind River Mountains are properly named. We passed south and westward to the country drained by the Humbodlt, by some called Mary's River. Saw Alkali Wells, with water even to the surface of the ground, but undrinkable. These holes are said to be unfathomable. We tied three long sticks together, with a heavy weight at one end and a thirty-foot rope at the other. Mr. Fuqua, who held the rope, thought he felt an under current.

The bracing atmosphere has given health to all, and caused "Pow" to dream of fresh meat. He told his dream at breakfast. Going to drive up the stock, I saw several deer running; fired two shots at the bunch at short range. Returning, I told them that I thought one was wounded. "Pow" found blood, and sure enough, trailed, killed and brought hams and saddle into camp. We often talked of that dream. Here we laid over for several days, caught fish, and turned up our noses at fried bacon, and I at black coffee.

A trip like this ought to make any man a judge of good horses, one of the best gifts of God to man. As a general rule, for endurance, large nostrils and sheth, with big barrel, fills the bill.

Coming down Humboldt River, our general course being southwest, water became worse and worse until the sink of Humboldt was reached. All grass and water permeated with alkali. With perpetual snow in sight we constantly dreamed of sweet water.

July 25. Arrived at the forty-five-mile desert. A man gave me a pint of water from Turkey River, the best drink I ever had. At 5 a. m. arrived at Carson River, just at daylight. The mules smelled water first and quickened their pace. In a half mile further we plainly felt the humidity in our faces. Trading post, by Californians, near the outcome of the desert. They sold water for twenty-five cents a quart, and a quarter section of dried apple pie for the same price.

Carson is the prettiest valley I ever saw. Viewed from the top of the mountains, with the river, like a silver thread meandering through, skirted here and there with trees and luxuriant alfalfa grass everywhere. Every mile or so sparkling branches run down the mountain side, from the west.

Stopped three days at Mormon station and enjoyed milk, pies, etc. The family is protected by a strong stockade. Traveled Johnson's Cut-Off over the mountains to Sacramento; sometimes too steep to ride comfortably, we drove the stock ahead, holding onto their tails. There was a little underbrush, and the soughing of the wind through the tall pine trees, and the resinous smell, reminded me of the Blue Ridge Mountains in Virginia. At night, looking across Carson Valley, many Indian camp fires could be seen far up the mountain side. Camped in sight of the Nevada Mountains and saw signs of grizzly bear. Some foot-packers have been keeping up with us for the last week. They are suffering for want of provisions. I am sorry that I cannot give them some, for I have barely enough to last me through. Came thirty-five miles today, passing through Placerville (Hangtown), and in three miles from Placerville reached Diamond Spring, in Eldorado County, California. Putting up at the hotel, we could not sleep comfortably in the house and slept out with the stock. Sold outfit to Mr. Argyle, my buckskin breeches bring me twenty dollars. Went by stage to Sacramento, and I foolishly riged out in broadcloth suit and plug hat, not knowing that people would take me for a preacher or a gambler, for these professions only dressed in style.

The journal ends thus: "I have written this journal partly in the day and partly at night, when it was raining, hailing, snowing—in all kinds of weather—therefore it contains many mistakes."

A year afterwards stopped at John Dawson's hotel in Sacramento City, on Fourth street, between J and K. Passing the parlors a fine looking lady hailed me, saying, "Mr. Terrell, don't you know me?" It was Cassie. She said that all were well, her brother Jo had made a fortune mining, and that she was keeping a boarding house. She had a baby in her lap—*its hair was red.*

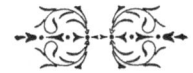

THE MASONIC BELL AT FORT WORTH.

When the writer came to Fort Worth, in 1857, he found a population of not exceeding 300 souls. The only pretentious structure in the embryo city was a lodge building of Fort Worth, No. 148, A. F. and A. Masons, a two-story brick building, used for Masonic and school purposes, and the worship of God by all denominations.

In Texas, as a general rule, Masonic buildings were erected first, and then came church edifices. This was because Masons were united and the church divided, as now, into many warring fragments, and thus it was and is, that Masonry smoothes into a harmonious whole the roughness caused by the bigotry and dissentions of the sects, and the selfishness, ignorance and ambition of their leaders.

Then the nearest chapter was distant a hundred miles. Many brethren traveled even a greater distance, through a country infested by Indians, to attend stated communications of this lodge. Then we were on the frontier, a small, poor and struggling band. Now we have the largest membership, and best equipped lodge building in the State, with flourishing Widows' and Orphans' Home built here by a donation of this lodge, and its friends, of not less than $9,000, raised and paid within the past two years.

Nothing recalls more vividly those times than the unusually sweet sounding bell located on the roof of the lodge building, and which often calls the craft to labor and refreshment.

There is something in the sound of the old bell that tenderly and softly recalls happy memories long forgotten, and keeps us in touch, as it were, with fellow-craftsmen whose spirits have returned to God. The shades of M. T. Johnson, Julian Fields, W. P. Burts, George Newman, the three Daggetts, Sam Sealy, Joel Snider, W. H. Overton, Lawrence Steele, John L. Purvis, W. T. Ferguson, H. C. Johnson, John Peter Smith, and a host of others rise up before us.

Who could but love, nay venerate, the inanimate obj..t

that conjures up such memories? No wonder old settlers love the bell; it rang out the old year, and rang in the new. It sounded the fire alarm, called to divine service, rang out merrily for weddings, and tolled dirges for their dead.

It was made in London in 1782, and was, in 1855, brought to Fort Worth, and owned by Lawrence Steele, who used it on the northwest corner of the public square, at his hotel, until 1871. Happily it escaped impressment, for bells were necessarily used during the Civil War for making cannon, and its remoteness from Richmond probably saved it.

In 1871 Oscar J. Lawrence and his sister, Miss Mary Victoria Lawrence taught the "Masonic Institute" in the old brick lodge building in this city, and they raised the money by public subscription to buy the bell for lodge and school purposes.

"Our much loved bell, our Mason bell,
    Could it but speak, true tales 'twould tell
Of youth and home, and those old times,
    When oft we heard your soothing chimes.

And so 'twill be, when we are gone,
    That tuneful peal will still ring on;
And other craftsmen to brothers tell
    And speak your praise, sweet Mason bell."

Long may our old bell be preserved to announce to the craft the hours of labor and rest.

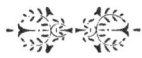

IN MEMORIAM.

Committee Report of A. F. and A. Masons Upon the Life and Death of J. P. Smith.

To the Worshipful Master, Warden and Brethren of Fort Worth Lodge 148, A. F. & A. Masons.

Brethren: Your committee appointed to draft a memorial and resolutions concerning the life and death of our beloved brother, John Peter Smith, deceased, beg leave to report as follows:

"His life was so gentle; and the elements
Were so mix'd in him, that Nature might stand up,
And say to all the world, THIS IS A MAN!"

On Thursday morning, April 11, 1901, John Peter Smith died in St. Louis, Mo., whither he had gone on business to further his life-work of upbuilding Texas and Fort Worth.

The announcement of his death caused a shock and thrill of unutterable regret to the entire community, by which he was so highly and universally respected and loved. All were our dear brother's friends. None, "none knew him but to love him, none named him but to praise."

After the shock had somewhat subsided we involuntarily asked ourselves the question "Gone? And shall we indeed see his familiar face no more, here where he lived doing good for forty-eight years; shall we be with him in the future life and there, with full identity, renew our love?"

The great mystery of life and death, known only to the Grand Architect, is hidden from man, whose finite mind can not fathom the cause of his creation nor the necessity of suffering and death.

We believe that if one worships God with all his heart, walks humbly before him, and does good and not evil, such an one will happily inherit eternal life.

Our dear departed brother loved and worshipped God and possessed in an unusual degree the Christian graces:

wherefore we have an abiding faith that we will by emulating his virtues, be reunited with him in "that house not made with hands, eternal in the heavens."

Brother John Peter Smith was early left an orphan, was a member and regular attendant of the Christian church services; was educated at Bethany College, Va.; was born in Owen County, Ky., September 16, 1831, and hence had nearly reached the three-score and ten limit. He located in Fort Worth, Texas, in 1853, and taught school here in 1854; was a surveyor and land locater by occupation; studied law here with A. Y. Fowler, and was admitted to the bar by Judge Nat J. Burford in 1860. In 1861 he voted against the ordinance of secession, but followed the fortunes of his State in the ensuing struggle. A member of Company K, Seventh regiment, Texas Cavalry, Silbley's Brigade, he participated in the campaign of New Mexico, Arizona and Western Louisiana; was severely wounded in 1863 near Donaldsonville, La., and slightly wounded at Mansfield; was present at the capture of Galveston in 1864; was adjutant of Greene's brigade; was promoted to colonel of his regiment near the close of the war, and disbanded his command in Navarro County in 1865.

In 1852-53 Brother Smith became a Mason, and was one of the original charter members of Fort Worth Lodge No. 148, which worked under dispensation in 1854, and was regularly chartered in 1855, our brother being secretary. He became a Royal Arch Mason in 1858, and served two years as High Priest of our Chapter. On the 4th of October, 1897, he was elected life member of this lodge, and exempted from all lodges dues. His mark is a coffin with sprig of acacia, recorded June 1, 1859. On the 16th of October, 1867, he was happily married to Mrs. Mary E. Fox, daughter of Col. James Young, in this county. Our brother and his wife taught the Masonic school here just after the close of the war. He leaves surviving him his dutiful and affectionate wife and five promising children, to-wit: James Young, John Peter, Florence C., William Beall, and Samuel C., the latter 16 years of age.

He was twice mayor of Fort Worth; caused the widening

of our sidewalks, the building of the gas and old water works, and was one of the eight who erected the Pickwick hotel, aided in building the Main street railway and cotton compress, donating to the city land for three cemeteries, besides making numerous private donations. He gave thousands of dollars to build our railways.

Although a man of mild and gentle manners, modest and unassuming, yet on occasion he could be firm and unyielding as adamant. When once he had fully investigated a subject he deferred his judgment to no man. In his domestic relations he was gentle, just, affectionate and most devoted. He was, indeed, a most lovable, useful and noble man. Long will his loss be felt by us and by all the community as well. Never can his place in our hearts be filled by another. He stands out, as it were, from all others as a fine example of old Texas manhood. For by his own effort and merits he rose from a poor, orphan boy, seeking on foot a home in the village of Fort Worth, to become one of the most useful and dearest beloved citizens of the State of Texas.

We recommend the passage of the following:

Resolved, By Fort Worth Lodge 148, Ancient, Free and Accepted Masons, that we deeply sympathize with the bereaved family of the deceased, and bow with submission and resignation to divine will in the taking of our beloved brother to Himself, where we hope to share with him eternal life.

Resolved, That the foregoing be spread on our book of records, and that a certified copy hereof, signed by the Worshipful Master, and attested by the secretary, be delivered to the family of the deceased.

J. C. Terrell,
T. N. Edgell,
C. D. Lusk,
Committee.

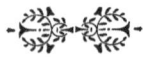

THE SOUL.

(BY JUDGE ALEX W. TERRELL.)

Like cosmic wreck from a distant sphere
  Is the erring human race—
Like atoms of dust we are drifting here
With blind unrest, and a haunting fear
  Of the tomb as a resting place.

We came to this world without our will,
  And will leave it with a sigh;
For the mingled threads of good and ill
In the warp of each life are weaving still,
  And will mingle till we die.

We may question the stars of our destiny—
  The stars with their clear, sweet light—
But the jeweled sky gives no reply
To the yearning spirit's plaintive cry
  In the stillness of the night.

From the mother's breast to the sexton's spade,
  There are tears—and toil—and strife—
If when this shell in the tomb is laid
Its soul like a flame burned out must fade—
  Why this hope for future life?

No token comes from beyond the tomb
  To tell if the soul is there;—
Does a falling star portend its doom—
A flash of light in the midnight gloom—
  Then darkness—everywhere?

No! No! There is something in us here
  That longs for a higher plane,—
An inborn hope for a brighter sphere
Where disenthralled from grief and fear
  We may live and love again.

This inborn hope illumes the way
  When life seems too hard to bear;
It was born with us,—and will ever stay
Like the star that heralds the dawn of day
  To keep us from despair.

If this hope deludes—then life is vain
  And cursed by an adverse fate;
If the soul can never live again
It's a curse more dread than the curse of Cain—
And our God—is a God of Hate.

No speck of matter around us here
  Is lost as the ages roll—
Can the breath of God, who rules this sphere,
Once breathed into man, now disappear?
  Can death destroy the soul?

Self-conscious, but viewless as the wind
  That churns the ocean foam,
The soul that is neither flesh nor mind—
With its subtle essence undefined,
  Keeps guard in its prison home.

And there like a watchful sentinel
  Its vigil in silence keeps;
But in whispered dreams will sometimes tell,
Cf a far off home where it longs to dwell,—
  For the spirit never sleeps.

The soul has never been seen nor heard,
  But lives to warn and to teach;
The fountain of tears by its touch is stirred—-
It quickens conscience without a word,
  Where silence is more than speech.

Does nothing exist that can't be seen,
   And that no man ever saw?
The earth in the spring is clothed in green,
   But who sees the *life* that gives it sheen?
      Or the Source of nature's law?

We call God "Father" because He made
   The living soul with His breath;
Can anger the Father's heart invade?
Does the Father still His child upbraid?
      Will He burn it after death?

Nothing but mystery here is found
   Where our senses feebly plod;
The mind constrained—by the finite bound—
Can never the depths of creation sound
      Nor fathom the ways of God.

No man-made creed can resolve our doubt—
   We are blind—and have always been,
But can *feel* when God directs our route
And the waiting soul with joy may shout
      With its faith in things unseen.

Faith is nursed by Hope in the realm of Love,
   Where her spirit wings are given;
When her trusting eyes are fixed above
She wings her way like an ark-bound dove
      To her destined home in heaven.

In this chequered life of pain and care
   Faith whispers to console,—
She can brave the storm with bosom bare,—
Or like breath of spring where roses are
      Can cheer the departing soul.

The parting soul will a helper need
   When it leaves this world of strife,—
But never a man with blood-stained creed,
For an angel plumed with love will lead
   When we pass from death to life.

Harmonious nature every hour
   Proclaims a Sentient Cause,—
Who wheels the planets,—paints the flower,—
And gives the soul its spirit power—
   CREATOR of nature's laws.

Oh! wonderful God! Thou art—nor can
   Thy love for Thy image fade;
Thou hast created the soul of man,—
No vengeful hate can distort Thy plan
   Nor destroy what Thou hast made.

In Thee—the Maker—I place my trust:—
   Thou didst not create in vain
This breathing clay—this pulsing dust,—
This home of tears and sensual lust,—
   This prison house of pain.

For pain is the tribute paid to bliss,
   And for future ecstasy.—
The death pang is nature's final kiss.—
The worm that dies in its chrysalis
   Revives with wings to fly.

Every soul while on earth renews some stain—
   Some sin—perhaps unconfessed:
But God will reclaim His own again. —
The crucified thief did not ask in vain,
   But in paradise is blessed.

To God my life was a written page—
  He knew all that I would be;—
He knew how the tyrant passions rage, —
How storm-swept is all my anchorage,—
  And why I would drift to sea.

I will trust Him in my utmost need
  To the resurrection morn;—
He knows that my every sinful deed
Was but ripened fruit from sin-germ seed
  That were sown ere I was born.

To free our souls from the taint of crime
  Christ died like a God for us;
His words still cheer as in olden time,
And the world's heart thrills in every clime
  To His tears for Lazarus.

I see God's love in the fragrant rose,—
  His strength in each wheeling sphere:
I feel His touch when the zephyr blows,—
His mercy for all like a river flows,
  And my soul has ceased to fear.

This trusting soul can ask for no more
  Than to keep its faith sublime:—
The loved and lost have gone before,
And wait for me on the restful shore
  That borders the stream of time.

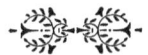

AN AFTERWORD.

When as a youth of twenty, J. C. Terrell left his family home in St. Joseph, Missouri, in May 1852 to seek his fortune in California, he had already been involved in numerous escapades, even for a young man of the mid-nineteenth century. He had just been admitted to the bar after attending the Kemper Family School (later Kemper Military Academy) at Boonville, Missouri, and reading law with his older brother, Alexander Terrell

While on the route overland, Terrell, during an idle moment, scratched his name and the date on a smooth stone. He later learned that passersby returning east had seen the stone and sent word to Terrell's family that he had died along the road and they had seen his tombstone. Because of the slowness of the mails in those times, it was quite a while before his family learned the truth. Terrell later often repeated the story to his children to illustrate the folly of writing one's name in public places.

He practiced law in Santa Clara and Monterrey for a few years, sailed up to Oregon briefly in 1856, then sailed 'round the Horn, returning to the States to visit his mother, who was living in Virginia. Travel was circuitous at best in those days, and, after visiting his brother Alexander (by then a resident of Austin, Texas), he took the stage from Austin to Fort Worth, on his way to make a stage connection to return to California. One of his traveling companions happened to be Middleton Tate Johnson who, only seven years before, had been one of the civilians guiding Major Ripley Arnold and Company "F" of the U.S. 2nd Dragoons to establish Fort Worth on the bluff above the Trinity River. Johnson was one of the biggest boosters of "Fort Town" and no doubt saw in the young Terrell the qualities that later made him such an asset to the fledgling community. However effective Johnson's sales pitch for Fort Worth, any thoughts of continuing to California were delivered the *coup de grâce* when, arriving in Fort Worth at Steele's Tavern, Terrell stepped off the stage and almost immediately ran into an old classmate, Dabney C. Dade, also now a young lawyer. Dade had come to Fort Worth and the Peters Colony the year before "to grow up with the country." Their law partnership was soon established in a two-room frame building at the corner of First and Main.

In Captain Terrell's day, the practice of law was much like the frontier: little formal precedent existed and much of one's success or failure depended more on strength of character than research and scholarship. Although it is fashionable to complain today about law and lawyers, such caviling is nothing new. William Shakespeare, almost five centuries ago, spoke of "the law's delays" and first penned the oft-(mis)quoted remark about "killing all the lawyers." While the bar of early Fort Worth may have had fewer laws and fewer lawyers to contend with, their court procedures were, by current standards, extremely arcane and cumbersome.

Not all of the legal practice in those days was bad, however. Lawyers were usually held in higher regard in the society of the day, customarily politely addressed as "Judge"—whether or not they ever held judicial office— again probably largely due to the character of the individuals who practiced law. Disillusionment or "burn-out" in the profession undoubtedly occurred, but surely in far fewer instances than today.

Terrell mentioned that no generation could write its own history. So it is with this slim volume. While many of the sketches are clearly first-hand, Terrell deftly minimizes his participation in the action, generally calling the attention to the acts of others to illustrate his point.

Terrell was a progenitor of what has always made Fort

Worth a premier and outstanding place to live, to work, to practice a profession. Possibly the genteel nature and small-town charm of living and working in Fort Worth is directly attributable to Terrell and his ilk.

Fort Worth has long sought to preserve a goodly measure of its frontier flavor and heritage. This publication of Terrell's reminiscences is such an undertaking. Parts of our past are well worth saving—to learn from and to emulate. Other parts are worth preserving in works like this— perhaps more to study, remember and guard against their return. Attributes and mores of one time and place may not and perhaps should not be easily transposed to another. Only by having the opportunity to study the first-hand memories, the unvarnished insights and thoughts of one such as Joseph C. Terrell do we have the means to make such a choice for ourselves.

Interestingly, this memoir is surprisingly silent in regard Captain Terrell's military service. Although an ardent Unionist and anti-secessionist, he nonetheless could not stand idly by once his adopted state went to war. In 1862, he raised a cavalry company and joined Waller's Battalion of Green's Brigade, taking part in several engagements in Louisiana. He refused promotions on several occasions, as promotion beyond captain would have meant separation from his men. After Appomattox, he returned to the practice of law in Fort Worth.

Terrell's reminiscences and, indeed, confessions, may reveal more about him and his age than he would have realized. The Captain's musings about reviving the whipping post might today be met with less than the universal approval they might have had in 1906 when this work was penned. Terrell was undoubtedly a man of sharp contrast, for he was, however, unquestionably far-sighted, socially progressive and benevolent. His own remarks of M. T. Johnson and E. M. Daggett (both giants of early Tarrant County), might well fit Captain Terrell as well:

Both were grand men, physically, morally and mentally. Neither were [sic] exemplary or saintly, yet both to us old settlers were veritable heroes. We loved them for the manifold good they did, and long years ago have buried their foibles.

Joseph Christopher Terrell married Miss Mary V. Lawrence in 1872. To this union were born five children, Sue A., John Lawrence, Josie C., Mary V., and Alexander W. Mary Lawrence Terrell died November 23, 1885. Captain Terrell married Miss Mary Peters Young on November 30, 1887. She died October 16, 1920. Captain Terrell died on October 15, 1909. Two of Captain Terrell's granddaughters—Josephine Terrell Hudson, daughter of Sue Terrell Hawley, and Catherine Terrell McCartney, daughter of John Lawrence Terrell—still live in Fort Worth.

Steve M. King, Judge
Probate Court Number One
Tarrant County, Texas